PARTY AND CLASS

The International Socialism book series (IS Books) aims to make available books that explain the theory and historical practice of working class self-emancipation from below. In so doing, we hope to rescue the main tenets of the revolutionary socialist tradition from its detractors on both the right and left. This is an urgent challenge for the left today, as we seek to rebuild this tradition in circumstances that often downplay the importance of organized revolutionaries.

By reissuing classics of the international socialist tradition, we hope to offer accessible and unique resources for today's generation of socialists.

Other titles in the International Socialism series:

PARTY AND CLASS

TONY CLIFF
DUNCAN HALLAS
CHRIS HARMAN
LEON TROTSKY

Haymarket Books
Chicago, Illinois

The first four chapters of this book were first published as *Party and Class* in 1971 by Pluto Press (London).

This expanded edition published in 2003 and 2017 by
Haymarket Books
P.O. Box 180165
Chicago, IL 60618
773-583-7884
www.haymarketbooks.org
info@haymarketbooks.org

ISBN: 978-1-60846-541-5

Trade distribution:
In the US, Consortium Book Sales and Distribution, www.cbsd.com
In Canada, Publishers Group Canada, www.pgcbooks.ca
In the UK, Turnaround Publisher Services, www.turnaround-uk.com
All other countries, Ingram Publisher Services International,
intlsales@perseusbooks.com

This book was published with the generous support of Lannan Foundation and Wallace Action Fund.

Printed in Canada by union labor.

Library of Congress Cataloging-in-Publication data is available.

10 9 8 7 6 5 4 3 2 1

This book is brought out in loving memory of Aaron Hess—a comrade who was lost to us far too soon. A committed revolutionary socialist for more than 20 years, Aaron embodied a spirit of political openness that inspired and challenged all those who knew him. Aaron had a rare ability to maintain a sense of historical and theoretical depth while remaining sensitive to new developments and willing to confront new problems with clear eyes. He would have wanted new generations of activists and socialists to be able to read and learn from this book, whose essays were written decades ago. He also would have wanted them to use what they learned to tackle the challenges facing socialists in the twenty-first century. We are honored to be able to dedicate a new printing of this book to him.

Contents

"Party and class" by Chris Harman was first published in *International Socialism*, first series, vol. 35, Winter 1968–9.

"Towards a revolutionary socialist party" by Duncan Hallas was first published in *Party and Class*, 1971.

"Trotsky on substitutionism" by Tony Cliff was first published in *International Socialism*, first series, vol. 2, Autumn 1960.

"The class, the party and the leadership" by Leon Trotsky was a manuscript found among his papers after his assasination and first published in *Party and Class*, 1971.

"What is sectarianism?" by Duncan Hallas was first published in *Education for Socialists*, 1985.

"Lenin and the revolutionary party" by Tony Cliff was first published in *International Socialism*, first series, vol. 58, May 1973.

Introduction

The problem of political organisation is as old as the socialist movement itself. Socialists, because their aim is to change the world, have always sought to organise themselves as effectively as possible in order to achieve this goal. The Hungarian Marxist Georg Lukacs pointed out that it is at the level of organisation that socialist ideas are put to the test of practice:[1] 'Every "theoretical" tendency or clash of views must immediately develop an organisational arm if it is to rise above the level of pure theory or abstract opinion, that is to say, if it really intends to point the way to its own fulfilment in practice.' But what is the best way to organise? How important is organisation? Are there some kinds of party structure that are an actual impediment to the attainment of socialist objectives?

These questions are particularly pressing for Marxists since Karl Marx conceived socialism as the self emancipation of the working class—it is, in other words, something working people must achieve for themselves. This implies the danger of what Leon Trotsky called 'substitutionism'— in other words, a would-be revolutionary party might seek to put itself in the place of the working class, seeking to take and hold power in its name. Marx and his collaborator Friedrich Engels specifically warned against this tendency in the socialist movement of their day, notably in the case of the followers of the French communist Auguste Blanqui who conceived revolution as a coup d'etat by a tiny group of conspirators.

Beyond, however, insisting that, in the words of the *Communist Manifesto*, 'the proletarian movement is the self conscious independent movement of the immense majority, in the interests of the immense majority,' Marx and Engels themselves did not pay systematic attention to the question of party organisation.[2] It was left to the Russian revolutionary leader Vladimir Lenin to place it at the centre of socialist

1

theory and practice. Discussing the problem of how the working class develops the consciousness necessary to overthrow capitalism, Lukacs wrote, 'Lenin was the first and for a long time the only leader and theoretician who tackled this problem at its theoretical roots and therefore at its decisive, practical point: *that of organisation*'.[3]

On no subject, however, has Lenin been a greater victim of distortion and vilification than with respect to the theory and practice of the revolutionary party. The historical orthodoxy that is emerging today, after the revolutions in Eastern Europe and the collapse of the Soviet Union, has essentially adopted the Cold War view of Lenin as an evil fanatic. In the work of veterans of the Cold War such as the right wing historian Richard Pipes and younger, more fashionable scholars such as Orlando Figes, he is depicted as the architect of a Bolshevik Party conceived from the start as an instrument of genocidal tyranny. The crimes of Stalinism can therefore be laid at Lenin's door. Thus Figes writes of Stalin: 'His drive towards industrialisation, sweeping aside the market and the peasantry, was in essence no different from Lenin's own drive towards Soviet power which had swept aside democracy'.[4]

In fact, the Russian Revolution of October 1917 was the most profoundly democratic event in history, the product of a revolutionary process driven by the spontaneous revolt of the oppressed and exploited and culminating in the Russian working class, organised through the Soviets of Workers' and Soldiers' Deputies, taking power. But they were only able to do so because of the leadership of the Bolshevik Party, not as a tight-knit band of middle class conspirators, but as a highly democratic mass workers' party. As Trotsky put it in his great *History of the Russian Revolution*, 'Without a guiding organisation, the energy of the masses would dissipate like steam not enclosed in a piston box. But nevertheless what moves things is not the piston or the box, but the steam'.[5]

It is true that the revolutionary energy of October 1917 did not last. Despite the efforts of the Bolsheviks to spread the revolution to the developed capitalist countries, the Russian soviet republic found itself isolated in a hostile capitalist world. Under the pressure of economic blockade and counter-revolutionary attack, the economy disintegrated, and with it the working class that had made the revolution. The Bolsheviks found themselves acting in the name of a working class that no longer existed. It was this real historical process that made possible the development of the Stalinist bureaucracy which usurped and betrayed October 1917.[6]

But the rise of Stalinism was precisely a *counter*-revolution, which destroyed everything that had been achieved by the October Revolution. The turning point in this process came with the forced collectivisation of agriculture in the late 1920s, and it culminated in the Great Terror of 1936-8, when the remnants of the old Bolshevik Party were slaughtered. The result was a society which had nothing to do with real socialism but was instead bureaucratic state capitalism, resting as surely on the exploitation of the working class as does its Western counterpart. Lenin died before this process was completed, but his last conscious political actions were in opposition to Stalin and what he represented. There is therefore a fundamental difference between Stalinism and Lenin's politics. He stood in the tradition of classical Marxism in which, as Marx put it, socialism is the self emancipation of the working class.

The four essays collected together here all concern themselves with, on the one hand, the relationship between working-class struggle and socialist organisation, and, on the other, the historical experience of the Russian Revolution and its aftermath. First published as a collection in 1971, they were in fact written at different times. It may help the reader to say something about the context in which each was composed, since it shaped the particular way they address the questions with which they are all concerned.

The oldest is Trotsky's essay, 'The class, the party and the leadership'. Unfinished at the time of his assassination by a Stalinist agent in August 1940, it is a response to attempts to explain the victory of the right under General Franco in the Spanish Civil War of 1936-9. Trotsky attacks the idea that defeat was inevitable because the Spanish working class was 'immature' and therefore supported the Communist Party and its Popular Front policies. He sees this as an attempt to absolve the main anti-Stalinist organisation in Spain, the Workers' Party of Marxist Unification (POUM), of its responsibility for effectively tailing these policies, with disastrous consequences not least for many POUM activists who perished at the hands of Stalin's or Franco's secret police.[7]

The essay is a powerful assertion of Trotsky's opposition to the vulgar distortion of historical materialism as a determinist doctrine in which events are the mechanical consequences of economic developments:

'Political leadership in the crucial moments of historical turns can become just as decisive a factor as is the role of the central command in the critical moments of war. History is not an automatic process. Otherwise, why leaders? Why parties? Why programmes? Why theoretical struggles?'

Political organisation is thus essential precisely because revolutions are not historically inevitable. At the same time Trotsky is careful to avoid the error often committed by sects claiming to act in his name of seeking to reduce every historical setback to the betrayals committed by the existing leadership of the workers' movement. He seeks to explain why workers remain so strongly attached to their traditional organisations which have proven themselves in the past. At the same time, he insists that great social crises put existing organisations to the test of responding to a rapidly developing class struggle and thus give small revolutionary parties the opportunity to win a mass following. The POUM's failure was that it did not seize this opportunity to shape events.

Tony Cliff's essay 'Trotsky on substititutionism' was first published when the Cold War was at its height in 1960. Then, as now, the ideological orthodoxy was that Leninism led ineluctably to Stalinism. Cliff takes as his starting point a famous remark of Trotsky's during the debates over organisation that surrounded the Second Congress of the Russian Social Democratic Workers Party in 1903, when the historic split between the Bolsheviks and the Mensheviks took place. At the time Trotsky sided with the Mensheviks in bitterly opposing Lenin's conception of a revolutionary vanguard party. He warned, 'These methods lead...to the Party organisation "substituting" itself for the Party, the Central Committee substituting itself for the Party organisation, and finally the dictator substituting himself for the Central Committee'.[8]

Trotsky of course later repudiated this diagnosis, joining the Bolsheviks in 1917 and becoming the main organiser of the October Revolution. But his remark is often seen as a prescient anticipation of what happened to the Bolsheviks and as a demonstration of the continuity between Lenin's conception of the party and the Stalinist system. Cliff seeks, however, to show that 'substitutionism'—the replacement of the working class by a revolutionary elite—is less an intellectual error than a social process. He demonstrates in some detail how it was the isolation of the revolution that caused the transformation of the Bolsheviks from a mass workers' party into an authoritarian regime ruling in the name of the proletariat. He also discusses the more general conditions under which substitutionism may arise, and concludes that the only real remedy for it is independent working-class activity.

The other two essays in this collection, by Duncan Hallas and Chris Harman, were written in very different political conditions. The upheavals of the late 1960s and early 1970s—above all the events of May-June 1968 in France—put revolutionary Marxism back on the political agenda. Tens of thousands of students and young workers in Western Europe and the Americas rallied to the banners of revolutionary organisations independent of both the Communist and the social democratic parties. The possibility of building genuine revolutionary parties capable of relating to rising workers' struggles was a real one.[9]

Unfortunately, misleading conceptions of party organisation tended to influence the new revolutionary generation. One, deriving from anarchists and semi-anarchist 'libertarian Marxists', accepted the Cold War consensus that Leninism led to Stalinism, and therefore repudiated any form of centralised party. Its mirror image prevailed among the various Maoist organisations that dominated the far left in continental Europe and North America. These adopted the Stalinist conception of the party as an omniscient monolith in which the masses should place their trust, and simply berated the Communist Parties as 'revisionists' that had failed to live up to this model. Such was the political confusion of the time that many moved quickly from semi-anarchist views to a Stalinist approach—and often, in disillusion, back again.

Harman's and Hallas's pieces both challenged these false conceptions and sought to win young revolutionaries to the genuine Leninist theory and practice of party building. In 'Towards A Revolutionary Socialist Party', which first appeared in 1971, Hallas concentrates his fire on two distortions of Leninism. The first is the classic anarchist critique of Bolshevism in the version presented by one of the leaders of the French students in May 1968, Daniel Cohn-Bendit, which particularly directs its fire at Trotsky as both leader and historian of the Russian Revolution.[10] The other is the tendency of orthodox Trotskyist groups—notably Gerry Healy's Socialist Labour League, the largest far left group in Britain in the 1950s and 1960s—simply to proclaim themselves the 'leadership' of the working class.[11]

Hallas insists instead on a realistic appraisal of the state of the workers' movement in Britain. He argues that the most important potential audience for revolutionaries is provided by the shop stewards, who then reflected the strength and self confidence of rank-and-file workers after more than 20 years of full employment. He notes that the dominant political influence on these workers is left reformism, in the shape of the Labour left and the Communist Party (then led by John Gollan), but that it is in decline, offering an opening through which revolutionary organisation can start to root itself among workers. In the event, the International Socialists (now the Socialist Workers Party) was only able to begin this process before it was cut short by the defeats workers suffered from the mid-1970s onwards. After nearly 20 years of Thatcherism rank-and-file workers have much less confidence in their ability to fight independently of the trade union bureaucracy. Nevertheless, Hallas's method—of starting from the actual balance of forces and the state of working-class consciousness—remains exemplary.

Finally, Chris Harman in 'Party and class' (first published in 1968) pursues the same debate through a broader exploration of divergent theoretical approaches. He argues that the reformist social democratic tradition tends to equate the revolutionary party with the working class itself (as, in a somewhat different way, does the Stalinist tradition). Even revolutionaries such as Trotsky (before 1917) and the great Polish Marxist Rosa Luxemburg tended to go along with this. Since a party of the whole class will reflect all the political currents among workers— conservative and even reactionary, as well as militant and revolutionary—it is likely to act as a brake on the struggle. Hence the tendency by both Luxemburg and the young Trotsky to regard party organisation as a force for conservatism and inertia.

Lenin and the Italian revolutionary Antonio Gramsci by contrast insisted on the sharp separation of party and class. The revolutionary party organises that section of the working class that accepts the basic principles of Marxism to win over the rest. Far from substituting itself for the class, it fights within workers' mass organisations to convince the majority that revolution is the only solution to its problems. Socialist revolution is thus, as Gramsci put it, 'the result of a dialectical process, in which the spontaneous movement of the revolutionary masses and the organising and directing will of the centre converge'.[12]

'Party and class' is a fundamental treatment of the problem of revolutionary organisation. It does, however, sometimes fall into a somewhat exclusive view of party membership, as Harman himself was the first to point out.[13] Thus he writes of the need 'to make its newest members rise to the level of understanding of its oldest'. But, often, if the party has been through a period in which there has been little mass struggle, the older members may, despite their formal understanding of Marxism, have become pessimistic and conservative because of the apparently thankless labour of holding the organisation together in unrevolutionary times. In these conditions, the new members recruited during a period of rising struggle, and therefore unscarred by this experience, bring with them an energy and enthusiasm that can revitalise the organisation.

For this reason also, Harman's call for 'a limitation' of party membership 'to those willing seriously and scientifically to appraise their own activity and that of the party generally' is excessively defensive. Sometimes it is necessary to 'open the gates of the party' and welcome in large numbers of newly radicalised workers, as Lenin argued the Bolsheviks should do during the 1905 Revolution. It nevertheless remains the case that, however radical these recruits may be when they join the party, they will only remain effective revolutionaries if, with the help of the older members, they gain a good grounding in the Marxist tradition and seek systematically to relate their practice to this theory, so that both are illuminated.

These minor weaknesses no doubt reflect the fact that 'Party and class' was written before the International Socialists began its first effort to root itself in the industrial working class, and before the Socialist Workers Party had to learn how to tack and turn in response to the ups and downs of the class struggle during the past 20 years. In this process the experience of the Bolsheviks between 1903 and 1917, although, of course, on a far larger scale and in very different conditions, has been invaluable. Tony Cliff's *Building the Party*, the first volume of his biography of Lenin (first published in 1975), is a detailed study of the theory and practice of revolutionary party building. It is an indispensable complement to the more theoretical essays published here.

All these essays, however, whatever the conditions of their original production, retain their relevance today. They serve to demonstrate the huge gap separating the genuine Marxist approach to revolutionary organisation from Stalinist despotism. And they provide a framework in which to address the problem of party building today. They can thus help to educate another generation in the theory and practice of revolutionary socialism.

1   G Lukacs, *History and Class Consciousness* (London, 1971), p299. The essay from which this quotation is taken, 'Towards a Methodology of the Problem of organisation', is a ground breaking discussion of the Leninist theory of the party.

2   K Marx and F Engels, *Collected Works*, VI (London, 1975), p495. See J Molyneux, *Marxism and the Party* (London, 1978), for an excellent discussion of this question, starting with Marx and Engels themselves.

3   G Lukacs, *Lenin* (London, 1970), p25. This little book is still the best single overview of Lenin's thought.

4   O Figes, *A People's Tragedy* (London, 1996), p815.

5   L Trotsky, *The History of the Russian Revolution*, 3 vols (London, 1967), Vol I, p17.

6   See C Harman, *Russia: How the Revolution was Lost* (London, 1969), T Cliff, *State Capitalism in Russia* (London, 1988), and A Callinicos, *The Revenge of History* (Cambridge, 1991), ch 3.

7   The issues involved are much more fully explored in L Trotsky, *The Spanish Revolution* (New York, 1973).

8   L Trotsky, *Our Political Tasks* (London, no date), p77. Cliff's fullest discussion of this controversy is in *Trotsky: Towards October 1879-1917* (London, 1989), chs. 3-5.

9   See C Harman, *The Fire Last Time* (London, 1988).

10   G Cohn-Bendit and D Cohn-Bendit, *Obsolete Communism: The Left-Wing Alternative* (Harmondsworth, 1969), Part IV.

11   For a discussion of this tendency see A Callinicos, *Trotskyism* (Milton Keynes, 1990), chs 2 and 3.

12   A Gramsci, *Selections from the Political Writings 1921-1926* (London, 1978), p198.

13   Author's Preface, C Harman, *Party and Class* (Chicago, 1986), pp4-5.

Party and class
Chris Harman

Few questions have produced more bitterness in Marxist circles than that of the relation between the party and the class. More heat has probably been generated in acrimonious disputes over this subject than any other. In generation after generation the same epithets are thrown about—'bureaucrat', 'substitutionist', 'elitist', 'autocrat'.

Yet the principles underlying such debate have usually been confused. This is despite the importance of the issues involved. For instance, the split between Bolsheviks and Mensheviks that occurred over the nature of the organisation of the party in 1903 found many of those who were to be on the opposite side of the barricades to Lenin in 1917 in his faction (for instance, Plekhanov), while against him were revolutionaries of the stature of Trotsky and Rosa Luxemburg. Nor was this confusion an isolated incident. It has been a continuous feature of revolutionary discussion. It is worth recalling Trotsky's remarks, at the Second Congress of the Comintern, in reply to Paul Levi's contention that the mass of workers of Europe and America understood the need for a party. Trotsky points out that the situation is much more complex than this. If the question is posed in the abstract:

> then I see Scheidemann on the one side and, on the other, American or French or Spanish syndicates who not only wish to fight against the bourgeoisie, but who, unlike Scheidemann, really want to tear its head off—for this reason I say that I prefer to discuss with these Spanish, American or French comrades in order to prove to them that the party is indispensable for the fulfilment of the historical mission which is placed upon them... I will try to prove this to them in a comradely way,

on the basis of my own experience, and not by counterposing to them Scheidemann's long years of experience saying that for the majority the question has already been settled... What is there in common between me and a Renaudel who excellently understands the need of the party, or an Albert Thomas and other gentlemen whom I do not even want to call 'comrades' so as not to violate the rules of decency?[1]

The difficulty to which Trotsky refers—that both social democrats and Bolsheviks refer to the 'need for a party', although what they mean by this are quite distinct things—has been aggravated in the years since by the rise of Stalinism. The vocabulary of Bolshevism was taken over and used for purposes quite opposed to those who formulated it. Yet too often those who have continued in the revolutionary tradition opposed to both Stalinism and social democracy have not taken Trotsky's points in 1920 seriously. They have often relied on 'experience' to prove the need for a party, although the experience is that of Stalinism and social democracy.

It will be the contention of this argument that most of the discussion even in revolutionary circles is, as a consequence, discussion for or against basically Stalinist or social democratic conceptions of organisation. It will be held that the sort of organisational views developed implicitly in the writings and actions of Lenin are radically different to both these conceptions. This has been obscured by the Stalinist debasement of the theory and practice of the October Revolution and the fact that the development of the Bolshevik Party took place under conditions of illegality and was often argued for in the language of orthodox social democracy.

The social democratic view of the relation of party and class

The classical theories of social democracy—which were not fundamentally challenged by any of the Marxists before 1914—of necessity gave the party a central role in the development towards socialism. For this development was seen essentially as being through a continuous and smooth growth of working-class organisation and consciousness under capitalism. Even those Marxists, such as Kautsky, who rejected the idea that there could be a gradual transition to socialism accepted that what was needed for the present was continually to extend organisational strength and electoral following. The growth of the party was essential so as to ensure that when the transition to socialism inevitably came, whether through elections or through defensive violence by the working class, the party capable of taking over and forming the basis of the new state (or the old one refurbished) would exist.

The development of a mass working-class party is seen as being an inevitable corollary of the tendencies of capitalist development. 'Forever greater grows the number of proletarians, more gigantic the army of superfluous labourers, and sharper the opposition between exploiters and exploited', crises 'naturally occur on an increasing scale', 'the majority of people sink ever deeper into want and misery', 'the intervals of prosperity become ever shorter; the length of the crises ever longer'. This drives greater numbers of workers 'into instinctive opposition to the existing order'. Social democracy, basing itself upon 'independent scientific investigation by bourgeois thinkers' exists to raise the workers to the level where they have a 'clear insight into social laws'.[2] Such a movement 'springing out of class antagonisms... cannot meet with anything more than temporary defeats, and must ultimately win'.[3] 'Revolutions are not made at will... They come with inevitable necessity.' The central mechanism involved in this development is that of parliamentary elections (although even Kautsky played with the idea of the General Strike in the period immediately after 1905-6).[4] 'We have no reason to believe that armed insurrection...will play a central role nowadays'.[5] Rather, 'it [parliament] is the most powerful lever that can be used to raise the proletariat out of its economic, social and moral degradation.'[6] The use of this by the working class makes 'parliamentarianism begin to change its character. It ceases to be a mere tool in the hands of the bourgeoisie'.[7] In the long run such activities must lead to the organisation of the working class and to a situation where the socialist party has the majority and will form the government. The Labour Party 'must have for its purpose the conquest of the government in the interests of the class it represents. Economic development will lead naturally to the accomplishment of this purpose'.[8]

Not only did this perspective lay the basis for most socialist action throughout western Europe in the 40 years prior to the First World War, it also went virtually unchallenged theoretically, at least from the left. Lenin's astonishment at the SPD's support for the war is well known. Not so often understood, however, is the fact that even left critics of Kautsky, such as Rosa Luxemburg, had not rejected the foundations of the theory of the relation of the party to the class and of the development of class consciousness implied. Their criticisms of Kautskyism tended to remain within the overall theoretical ground provided by Kautskyism.

What is central for the social democrat is that the party *represents* the class. Outside of the party the worker has no consciousness. Indeed, Kautsky himself seemed to have an almost pathological fear of what the workers would do without the party and of the associated dangers of a 'premature' revolution. Thus it had to be the party that takes power. Other forms of working-class organisation and activity can help, but must be subordinated to the bearer of political consciousness. 'This "direct action" of the unions can operate effectively only as an auxiliary and reinforcement to and not as a substitute for parliamentary action.'[9]

The revolutionary left and social democratic theories

No sense can be made of any of the discussions that took place in relation to questions of organisation of the party prior to 1917 without understanding that this social democratic view of the relation of party and class was *nowhere* explicitly challenged (except among the anarchists who rejected any notion of a party). Its assumptions were shared even by those, such as Rosa Luxemburg, who opposed orthodox social democracy from the point of view of mass working-class self activity. This was not a merely theoretical failing. It followed from the historical situation. The Paris Commune was the only experience then of working-class power, and that had been for a mere two months in a predominantly petty bourgeois city. Even the 1905 revolution gave only the most embryonic expression of how a workers' state would in fact be organised. The fundamental forms of workers' power—the soviets (workers' councils)—were not recognised. Thus Trotsky, who had been president of the Petrograd Soviet in 1905, does not mention them in his analysis of the lessons of 1905, *Results and Prospects*. Virtually alone in foreseeing the socialist content of the Russian Revolution, Trotsky did not begin to see the form this would take:

> Revolution is first and foremost a question of power—not of the state form (constituent assembly, republic, united states) but of the social content of the government.[10]

There was a similar omission in Rosa Luxemburg's response to 1905, *The Mass Strike*. Not until the February revolution did soviets become central in Lenin's writings and thoughts.[11]

The revolutionary left never fully accepted Kautsky's position of seeing the party as the direct forerunner of the workers' state. Luxemburg's writings, for instance, recognise the conservatism of the party and the need for the masses to go beyond and outside it from a very early stage.[12] But there is never an explicit rejection of the official social democratic position. Yet without the theoretical clarification of the relationship between the party and the class there could be no possibility of clarity over the question of the necessary internal organisation of the party. Without a rejection of the social democratic model, there could not be the beginnings of a real discussion about revolutionary organisation.

This is most clearly the case with Rosa Luxemburg. It would be wrong to fall into the trap (carefully laid by both Stalinists and would-be followers of Luxemburg) of ascribing to her a theory of 'spontaneity' that ignores the need for a party. Throughout her writings there is stress upon the need for a party and the positive role it must play:

> In Russia, however, the social democratic party must make up by its own efforts an entire historical period. It must lead the Russian proletarians from their present 'atomised' condition, which prolongs the autocratic regime, to a class organisation that would help them to become aware of their historical objectives and prepare them to struggle to achieve those objectives.[13]
>
> ...The task of social democracy does not consist in the technical preparation and direction of mass strikes, but first and foremost in the political leadership of the whole movement.[14]
>
> The social democrats are the most enlightened, the most class-conscious vanguard of the proletariat. They cannot and dare not wait, in a fatalistic fashion with folded arms for the advent of the 'revolutionary situation'.[15]

Yet there is a continual equivocation in Luxemburg's writings on the role of the party. She was concerned that the leading role of the party should not be too great—for she identified this as 'the prudent position of social democracy'. She identified 'centralism', which she saw as anyway necessary ('the social democracy is, as a rule, hostile to any manifestation of localism or federalism') with the 'conservatism inherent in such an organ (ie the Central Committee)'.[16] Such equivocation cannot be understood without taking account of the concrete situation Luxemburg was really concerned about. She was a leading member of the SPD, but was always uneasy about its mode of operation. When she really wanted to illustrate the dangers of centralism it was to this that she referred:

> The present tactical policy of the German social democracy has won universal esteem because it is supple as well as firm. This is a sign of the fine adaptation of our party to the conditions of a parliamentary regime... However, the very perfection of this adaptation is already closing vaster horizons to our party.[17]

Brilliantly prophetic as this is of what was to happen in 1914, she does not begin to explain the origins of the increasing sclerosis and ritualism of the SPD, let alone indicate ways of fighting this. Conscious individuals and groups cannot resist this trend. For 'such inertia is due, to a large degree, to the fact that it is inconvenient to define, within the vacuum of abstract hypotheses, the lines and forms of non-existent political situations'.[18] Bureaucratisation of the party is seen as an inevitable phenomenon that only a limitation on the degree of cohesion and efficiency of the party can overcome.

It is not a particular form of organisation and conscious direction, but organisation and conscious direction as such that limit the possibilities for the 'self conscious movement of the majority in the interests of the majority':

> The unconscious comes before the conscious. The logic of history comes before the subjective logic of the human beings who participate in the historic process. The tendency is for the directing organs of the socialist party to play a conservative role.[19]

There is a correct and important element in this argument: the tendency for certain sorts of organisations to be unable (or unwilling) to respond to a rapidly changing situation. One only has to think of the maximalist wing of the Italian Socialist Party in 1919, the whole of the 'centre' of the Second International in 1914, the Menshevik-Internationalists in 1917, or the KPD (German Communist Party) in 1923. Even the Bolshevik Party contained a very strong tendency to exhibit such conservatism. But Luxemburg, having made the diagnosis, makes no attempt to locate its source, except in epistemological generalities, or looks for organisational remedies. There is a strong fatalism in her hope that the 'unconscious' will be able to correct the 'conscious'. Despite her superb sensitivity to the peculiar tempo of development of the mass movement, particularly in *The Mass Strike*, she shies away from trying to work out a clear conception of the sort of political organisation that can harness such spontaneous developments. Paradoxically this most trenchant critic of bureaucratic ritualism and parliamentary cretinism argued in the 1903 debate for precisely that faction of the Russian party that was to be the most perfected historical embodiment of these failings: the Mensheviks. In Germany political opposition to Kautskyism, which was already developing at the turn of the century and was fully formed by 1910, did not take on concrete organisational forms for another five years.

Considerable parallels exist between Luxemburg's position and that which Trotsky adheres to up to 1917. He too is very aware of the danger of bureaucratic ritualism:

> The work of agitation and organisation among the ranks of the proletariat has an internal inertia. The European socialist parties, particularly the largest of them, the German Social Democratic Party, have developed an inertia in proportion as the great masses have embraced socialism and the more these masses have become organised and disciplined. As a consequence of this, social democracy as an organisation embodying the political experience of the proletariat may at a certain moment become a direct obstacle to open conflict between the workers and bourgeois reaction.[20]

Again his revolutionary spirit leads him to distrust all centralised organisation. Lenin's conception of the party can, according to Trotsky in 1904, only lead to the situation in which:

> The organisation of the party substitutes itself for the party as a whole; then the central committee substitutes itself for the organisation; and finally the 'dictator' substitutes himself for the central committee.[21]

But for Trotsky the real problems of working-class power can only be solved:

> by way of systematic struggle between...many trends inside socialism, trends which will inevitably emerge as soon as the proletarian dictatorship poses tens and hundreds of new...problems. No strong 'domineering' organisation will be able to suppress these trends and controversies.[22]

Yet Trotsky's fear of organisational rigidity leads him also to support that tendency in the inner party struggle in Russia which was historically to prove itself most frightened by the spontaneity of mass action. Although he was to become increasingly alienated from the Mensheviks politically, he did not begin to build up an organisation in opposition to them until very late. Whether he was correct or not in his criticisms of Lenin in 1904 (and we believe he was wrong), he was only able to become an effective historical actor in 1917 by joining Lenin's party.

If organisation does produce bureaucracy and inertia, Luxemburg and the young Trotsky were undoubtedly right about the need to limit the aspirations towards centralism and cohesion among revolutionaries. But it is important to accept all the consequences of this position. The most important must be a historical fatalism. Individuals can struggle among the working class for their ideas, and these ideas can be important in giving workers the necessary consciousness and confidence to fight for their own liberation. But revolutionaries can never build the organisation capable of giving them effectiveness and cohesion in action comparable to that of those who implicitly accept present ideologies. For to do so is inevitably to limit the self activity of the masses, the 'unconscious' that precedes the 'conscious'. The result must be to wait for 'spontaneous' developments among the masses. In the meantime one might as well put up with the organisations that exist at present, even if one disagrees with them politically, as being the best possible, as being the maximum present expression of the spontaneous development of the masses.

Lenin and Gramsci on the party and the class

In the writings of Lenin there is an ever present implicit recognition of the problems that worry Luxemburg and Trotsky so much. But there is not the same fatalistic succumbing to them. There is an increasing recognition that it is not organisation as such, but particular forms and aspects of organisation that give rise to these. Not until the First World War and then the events in 1917 gave an acute expression to the faults of old forms of organisation did Lenin begin to give explicit notice of the radically new conceptions he himself was developing. Even then these were not fully developed. The destruction of the Russian working class, the collapse of any meaningful *Soviet* system (ie one based upon real workers' councils), and the rise of Stalinism, smothered the renovation of socialist theory. The bureaucracy that arose with the decimation and

demoralisation of the working class took over the theoretical foundations of the revolution, to distort them into an ideology justifying its
own interests and crimes. Lenin's view of what the party is, and how it
should function in relation to the class and its institutions, was no sooner
defined against older social democratic conceptions with some clarity
than it was again obscured by a new Stalinist ideology.

Many of Lenin's conceptions are, however, taken up and given clear
and coherent theoretical form by the Italian Antonio Gramsci.[23]

What is usually ignored by commentators on Lenin is that throughout
his writings are two intertwined and complementary conceptions, which
to the superficial observer seem contradictory. Firstly there is continual
stress on the possibilities of sudden transformations of working-class
consciousness, on the unexpected upsurge that characterises working-
class self activity, on deep rooted instincts in the working class that lead
it to begin to reject habits of deference and subservience:

> In...the history of revolutions there come to light contradictions that have
> ripened for decades and centuries. Life becomes unusually eventful. The
> masses, which have always stood in the shade and therefore have often
> been despised by superficial observers, enter the political arena as active
> combatants... These masses are making heroic efforts to rise to the occa-
> sion and cope with the gigantic tasks of world significance imposed upon
> them by history; and however great individual defeats may be, however
> shattering to us the rivers of blood and the thousands of victims, nothing
> will ever compare in importance with this direct training that the masses
> and the classes receive in the course of the revolutionary struggle itself.[24]
>
> We are able to appreciate the importance of the slow, steady and often
> imperceptible work of political education which social democrats have
> always conducted and always will conduct. But we must not allow what
> in the present circumstances would be still more dangerous—a lack of
> faith in the powers of the people. We must remember what a tremendous
> educational and organisational power the revolution has, when mighty
> historical events force the man in the street out of his remote garret or
> basement corner, and make a citizen of him. Months of revolution some-
> times educate citizens more quickly and fully than decades of political
> stagnation.[25]
>
> The working class is instinctively, spontaneously social democratic.[26]
>
> The special condition of the proletariat in capitalistic society leads
> to a striving of workers for socialism; a union of them with the socialist

party bursts forth with a spontaneous force in the very early stages of the movement.[27]

Even in the worst months after the outbreak of war in 1914 he could write:

The objective war-created situation...is inevitably engendering revolutionary sentiments; it is tempering and enlightening all the finest and most class conscious proletarians. A sudden change in the mood of the masses is not only possible, but is becoming more and more probable.[28]

In 1917 this faith in the masses leads him in April and in August-September into conflict with his own party:

Lenin said more than once that the masses are to the left of the party. He knew the party was to the left of its own upper layer of 'old Bolsheviks'.[29]

In relation to the 'Democratic Conference' he can write:

We must draw the masses into the discussion of this question. Class conscious workers must take the matter into their own hands, organise the discussion and exert pressure on 'those at the top'.[30]

There is, however, a second fundamental element in Lenin's thought and practice: the stress on the role of theory and of the party as the bearer of this. The most well known recognition of this occurs in *What is to be Done?* when Lenin writes that 'without revolutionary theory there can be no revolutionary practice'.[31] But it is the theme that recurs at every stage in his activities, not only in 1903, but also in 1905 and 1917 at exactly the same time as he was cursing the failure of the party to respond to the radicalisation of the masses. And for him the party is something very different from the mass organisations of the whole class. It is always a vanguard organisation, membership of which requires a dedication not to be found in most workers. (But this does not mean that Lenin ever wanted an organisation only of professional revolutionaries.)[32] This might seem a clear contradiction, particularly as in 1903 Lenin uses arguments drawn from Kautsky which imply that only the party can imbue the class with a socialist consciousness, while later he refers to the class being more 'to the left' than the party. In fact, however, to see a contradiction here is to fail to understand the fundamentals of Lenin's thinking on these issues. For the real theoretical basis for his argument on the party is not that the working class is incapable on its own of coming to theoretical socialist consciousness. This Lenin admits at the Second Congress of the RSDLP when he denies that 'Lenin takes no account whatever of the fact that the workers too have a share in the formation of an ideology' and adds that 'the "economists" have gone to one extreme. To straighten matters out somebody had to pull in the other direction—and that is what I have done'.[33]

The real basis for his argument is that the level of consciousness in the working class is never uniform. However rapidly the mass of workers learn in a revolutionary situation, some sections will still be more advanced than others. To merely take delight in the spontaneous transformation is to accept uncritically whatever transitory products this throws up. But these reflect the backwardness of the class as well as its movement forward, its situation in bourgeois society as well as its potentiality of further development so as to make a revolution. Workers are not automatons without ideas. If they are not won over to a socialist world view by the intervention of conscious revolutionaries, they will continue to accept the bourgeois ideology of existing society. This is all the more likely because it is an ideology that flavours all aspects of life at present and is perpetuated by all media. Even if some workers were 'spontaneously' to come to a fully fledged scientific standpoint they would still have to argue with others who had not:

> To forget the distinction between the vanguard and the whole of the masses gravitating towards it, to forget the vanguard's constant duty of raising ever wider sections to its own advanced level, means simply to deceive oneself, to shut one's eyes to the immensity of our tasks, and to narrow down these tasks.[34]

This argument is not one that can be restricted to a particular historical period. It is not one, as some people would like to argue, that applies to the backward Russian working class of 1902 but not to those in the advanced countries today. The absolute possibilities for the growth of working-class consciousness may be higher in the latter, but the very nature of capitalist society continues to ensure a vast unevenness within the working class. To deny this is to confuse the revolutionary *potential* of the working class with its present situation. As he writes against the Mensheviks (and Rosa Luxemburg!) in 1905:

Use fewer platitudes about the development of the independent activity of the workers—the workers display no end of independent revolutionary activity which you do not notice!—but see to it rather that you do not demoralise undeveloped workers by your own tailism.[35]

...There are two sorts of independent activity. There is the independent activity of a proletariat that possesses revolutionary initiative, and there is the independent activity of a proletariat that is undeveloped and held in leading strings... There are social democrats to this day who contemplate with reverence the second kind of activity, who believe they can evade a direct reply to pressing questions of the day by repeating the word 'class' over and over again.[36]

In short, stop talking about what the class as a whole can achieve and start talking about how we as part of its development are going to act. As Gramsci writes:

Pure spontaneity does not exist in history, it would have to coincide with pure mechanical action. In the 'most spontaneous' of movements the elements of 'conscious direction' are only uncontrollable... There exists a multiplicity of elements of conscious direction in these movements, but none of them is predominant.[37]

Human beings are never without some conception of the world. They never develop apart from some collectivity. 'For his conception of the world a man always belongs to some grouping, and precisely to that of all the social elements who share the same way of thinking and working'—unless he is involved in a constant process of criticism of his world view so as to give it coherence:

He belongs simultaneously to a multiplicity of men-masses, his own personality is made up in a queer way. It contains elements of the caveman and principles of the most modern advanced learning, shabby prejudices of all past historical phases, and intuitions of a future philosophy of the human race united all over the world.[38]

... The active man of the masses works practically, but does not have a clear theoretical consciousness of his actions, which is also a knowledge of the world insofar as he changes it. Rather his theoretical consciousness may be opposed to his actions. We can almost say that he has two theoretical consciousnesses (or one contradictory consciousness), one implicit in his actions, which unites him with all his colleagues in the practical transformation of reality, and one superficially explicit or verbal which

he has inherited from the past and which he accepts without criticism...
[This division can reach the point] where the contradiction within his
consciousness will not permit any action, any decision, any choice, and
produces a state of moral and political passivity.[39]

All action is the result of diverse wills affected with a varying degree
of intensity, of consciousness, of homogeneity with the entire mass of the
collective will... It is clear that the corresponding, implicit theory will be
a combination of beliefs and points of view as confused and heterogeneous. [If practical forces released at a certain historical point are to be]
effective and expansive [it is necessary to] construct on a determined
practice a theory that coinciding with and being identified with the decisive elements of the same practice, accelerates the historical process in
act, makes the practice more homogeneous, coherent, more efficacious in
all its elements.[40]

In this sense the question as to the preferability of 'spontaneity' or
'conscious direction' becomes that of whether it is:

preferable to think without having a critical awareness, in a disjointed
and irregular way, in other words to 'participate' in a conception of the
world 'imposed' mechanically by the external environment, that is by one
of the many social groups in which everyone is automatically involved
from the time he enters the conscious world, or is it preferable to work
out one's own conception of the world consciously and critically.[41]

Parties exist in order to act in this situation to propagate a particular
world view and the practical activity corresponding to it. They attempt
to unite together into a collectivity all those who share a particular world
view and to spread this. They exist to give homogeneity to the mass of
individuals influenced by a variety of ideologies and interests. But they
can do this in two ways.

The first Gramsci characterises as that of the Catholic Church. This
attempts to bind a variety of social classes and strata to a single ideology. It attempts to unite intellectuals and 'ordinary people' in a single
organised world view. But it can only do this by an iron discipline over
the intellectuals that reduces them to the level of the 'ordinary people'.
'Marxism is antithetical to this Catholic position.' Instead it attempts to
unite intellectuals and workers so as to constantly raise the level of consciousness of the masses, so as to enable them to act truly independently.
This is precisely why Marxists cannot merely 'worship' the spontaneity of

the masses: this would be to copy the Catholics in trying to impose on the most advanced sections the backwardness of the least.

For Gramsci and Lenin this means that the party is constantly trying to make its newest members rise to the level of understanding of its oldest. It has always to be able to react to the 'spontaneous' developments of the class, to attract those elements that are developing a clear consciousness as a result of these:

> To be a party of the masses not only in name, we must get ever wider masses to share in all party affairs, steadily to elevate them from political indifference to protest and struggle, from a general spirit of protest to an adoption of social democratic views, from adoption of these views to support of the movement, from support to organised membership in the party.[42]

The party able to fulfil these tasks will not, however, be the party that is necessarily 'broadest'. It will be an organisation that combines a constant attempt to involve in its work ever wider circles of workers with a limitation on its membership to those willing to seriously and scientifically appraise their own activity and that of the party generally. This necessarily means that the definition of what constitutes a party member is important. The party is not to be made up of just anybody wishing to belong to it, but only those willing to accept the discipline of its organisations. In normal times the numbers of these will be only a relatively small percentage of the working class; but in periods of upsurge they will grow immeasurably.

There is an important contrast here with the practice in social democratic parties. Lenin himself realises this only insofar as Russia is concerned prior to 1914, but his position is clear. He contrasts his aim—a 'really iron strong organisation', a 'small but strong party' of 'all those who are out to fight'—with the 'sprawling monster, the new-*Iskra* motley elements of the Mensheviks'.[43] This explains his insistence on making a principle out of the question of the conditions for membership of the party when the split with the Mensheviks occurred.

Within Lenin's conception those elements that he himself is careful to regard as historically limited and those of general application must be distinguished. The former concern the stress on closed conspiratorial organisations and the need for careful direction from the top down of party officials, etc.

Under conditions of political freedom our party will be built entirely on the elective principle. Under the autocracy this is impracticable for the collective thousands of workers that make up the party.[44]

Of much more general application is the stress on the need to limit the party to those who are going to accept its discipline. It is important to stress that for Lenin (as opposed to many of his would-be followers) this is not a blind acceptance of authoritarianism. The revolutionary party exists so as to make it possible for the most conscious and militant workers and intellectuals to engage in scientific discussion as a prelude to concerted and cohesive action. This is not possible without general participation in party activities. This requires clarity and precision in argument combined with organisational decisiveness. The alternative is the 'marsh'—where elements motivated by scientific precision are so mixed up with those who are irremediably confused as to prevent any decisive action, effectively allowing the most backward to lead. The discipline necessary for such a debate is the discipline of those who have 'combined by a freely adopted decision'.[45] Unless the party has clear boundaries and unless it is coherent enough to implement decisions, discussion over its decisions, far from being 'free', is pointless. Centralism for Lenin is far from being the opposite of developing the initiative and independence of party members; it is the precondition of this. It is worth noting how Lenin summed up the reasons for his battle for centralism over the previous two years in 1905. Talking of the role of the central organisation and of the central paper he says that the result was to be the:

> creation of a network of agents...that...would not have to sit round waiting for the call to insurrection, but would carry out such regular activity that would guarantee the highest probability of success in the event of an insurrection. Such activity would strengthen our connections with the broadest masses of the workers and with all strata that are discontented with the aristocracy... Precisely such activity would serve to cultivate the ability to estimate correctly the general political situation and, consequently, the ability to select the proper moment for the uprising. Precisely such activity would train all local organisations to respond simultaneously to the same political questions, incidents, and events that agitate the whole of Russia and to react to these 'incidents' in the most rigorous, uniform and expedient manner possible.[46]

By being part of such an organisation, worker and intellectual alike are trained to assess their own concrete situation in accordance with the scientific socialist activity of thousands of others. 'Discipline' means acceptance of the need to relate individual experience to the total theory and practice of the party. As such it is not opposed to, but a necessary prerequisite of, the ability to make independent evaluations of concrete situations. That is also why 'discipline' for Lenin does not mean hiding differences that exist within the party, but rather exposing them to the full light of day so as to argue them out. Only in this way can the mass of members make scientific evaluations. The party organ must be open to the opinions of those it considers inconsistent:

> It is necessary in our view to do the utmost—even if it involves certain departures from tidy patterns of centralism and from absolute obedience to discipline—to enable these grouplets to speak out and give the whole party the opportunity to weigh the importance or unimportance of those differences and to determine where, how and on whose part inconsistency is shown.[47]

In short, what matters is that there is political clarity and hardness in the party so as to ensure that all its members are brought into its debate and understand the relevance of their own activity. That is why it is absurd, as the Mensheviks tried to do, and as some people still do, to confuse the party with the class. The class as a whole is constantly engaged in unconscious opposition to capitalism; the party is that section of it that is already conscious and unites to try to give conscious direction to the struggle of the rest. Its discipline is not something imposed from the top downwards, but rather something that is voluntarily accepted by all those who participate in its decisions and act to implement these.

The social democratic party, the Bolshevik Party and the Stalinist party

We can now see the difference between the party as Lenin conceived it and the social democratic party simultaneously envisaged and feared by Rosa Luxemburg and Trotsky. The latter was thought of as a party of the whole class. The coming to power of the class was to be the party taking power. All the tendencies within the class had to be represented within it. Any split within it was to be conceived of as a split within the class. Centralisation, although recognised as necessary, was feared as a centralisation over and against the spontaneous activity of the class. Yet it was precisely in this sort of party that the 'autocratic' tendencies warned against by Luxemburg were to develop most. For within it the confusion of member and sympathiser, the massive apparatus needed to hold together a mass of only half-politicised members in a series of social activities, led to a toning down of political debate, a lack of political seriousness, which in turn reduced the ability of the members to make independent political evaluations and increased the need for apparatus-induced involvement. Without an organisational centralisation aimed at giving clarity and decisiveness to political differences, the independence of the rank-and-file members was bound to be permanently undermined. Ties of personal affection or of deference to established leaders become more important than scientific, political evaluation. In the marsh, where no one takes a clear road, even if the wrong one, then there is no argument as to which is the right one. Refusal to relate organisational ties to political evaluations, even if done under the noble intention of maintaining a 'mass party', necessarily led to organisational loyalties replacing political ones. This in turn entailed a failure to act independently given opposition from old colleagues (the clearest example of this tendency was undoubtedly Martov in 1917).

It is essential to understand that the Stalinist party is not a variant of the Bolshevik Party. It too was dominated by organisational structures. Adherence to the *organisation* rather than to the politics of the organisation mattered. Theory existed to justify an externally determined practice, not vice versa. Organisational loyalties of the apparatus are responsible for political decisions (the former relate in turn to the needs of the Russian state apparatus). It is worth noting that in Russia a real victory of the apparatus over the party required precisely the bringing into the party of hundreds of thousands of 'sympathisers', a dilution of the 'party' by the 'class'. At best politically unsure of themselves, the 'Lenin levy' could be relied upon to defer to the apparatus. The Leninist party does not suffer from this tendency to bureaucratic control precisely because it restricts its membership to those willing to be serious and disciplined enough to take *political* and *theoretical* issues as their starting point, and to subordinate all their activities to these.

But does this not imply a very elitist conception of the party? In a sense it does, although this is not the fault of the party, but of life itself, which gives rise to an uneven development of working-class consciousness. The party to be effective has to aim at recruiting all those it conceives of as being most 'advanced'. It cannot reduce its own level of science and consciousness merely in order not to be an 'elite'. It cannot, for instance, accept that chauvinist workers are 'as good as' international-ist party members, so as to take account of the 'self activity' of the class. But to be a 'vanguard' is not the same as to substitute one's own desires, or policies or interests, for those of the class.

Here it is important to see that for Lenin the party is not the embryo of the workers' state—the workers' council is. The working class as a whole will be involved in the organisations that constitute its state, the most backward as well as the most progressive elements. 'Every cook will govern.' In Lenin's major work on the state, the party is hardly men-tioned. The function of the party is not to be the state, but rather to carry out continual agitation and propaganda among more backward elements of the class so as to raise their self consciousness and self reliance to the pitch that they will both set up workers' councils and fight to overthrow the forms of organisation of the bourgeois state. The soviet state is the highest concrete embodiment of the self activity of the whole working class; the party is that section of the class that is most conscious of the world historical implications of this self activity.

The functions of the workers' state and of the party should be quite different (which is why there can be more than one party in a workers' state). One has to represent all the diverse interests of all the sections—geographical, industrial, etc—of the workers. It has to recognise in its mode of organisation all the heterogeneity of the class. The party, on the other hand, is built around those things that unite the class nation-ally and internationally. It constantly aims, by ideological persuasion, to overcome the heterogeneity of the class. It is concerned with national and international political principles, not parochial concerns of indi-vidual groups of workers. It can only persuade, not coerce these into accepting its lead. An organisation that is concerned with participating in the revolutionary overthrow of capitalism by the working class cannot conceive of substituting itself for the organs of direct rule of that class. Such a perspective is only available to the social democratic or Stalinist party (and both have been too afraid of mass self activity to attempt this substitution through revolutionary practice in advanced capitalist coun-tries). Existing under capitalism, the revolutionary organisation will of necessity have a quite different structure to that of the workers' state that will arise in the process of overthrowing capitalism.[48] The revolutionary party will have to struggle within the institution of the workers' state for its principles as against those with opposed ones; this is only possible because it itself is not the workers' state.[49]

This enables us to see that Lenin's theory of the party and his theory of the state are not two separate entities, capable of being dealt with in isolation from one another. Until he developed the theory of the state, he tended to regard the Bolshevik Party as a peculiar adaptation to Russian circumstances. Given the social democratic (and later the Stalinist) conception of the party becoming the state, it is only natural for genuinely revolutionary and therefore democratic socialists not to want to restrict the party to the most advanced sections of the class, even if the need for such an organisation of the most conscious sections is recognised. This explains Rosa Luxemburg's ambiguity over the question of political organisation and theoretical clarity. It enables her to counterpose the 'errors committed by a truly revolutionary movement' to the 'infallibility of the cleverest Central Committee'. But if the party and the institutions of class power are distinct (although one attempts to influence the other) the 'infallibility' of the one is a central component in the process by which the other learns from its errors. It is Lenin who sees this. It is Lenin who draws the lessons, not (at least until the very end of her life) Luxemburg. It is not true that, 'for Marxists in the advanced industrial countries, Lenin's original position can much less serve as a guide than Rosa Luxemburg's...'[50] The need is still to build an organisation of revolutionary Marxists that will subject their situation and that of the class as a whole to scientific scrutiny, will ruthlessly criticise their own mistakes, and will, while engaging in the everyday struggles of the mass of workers, attempt to increase their independent self activity by unremittingly opposing their ideological and practical subservience to the old society. A reaction against the identification of class and party elite made by both social democracy and Stalinism is very healthy. It should not, however, prevent a clear-sighted perspective of what we have to do to overcome their legacy.

1   L Trotsky, *The First Five Years of the Communist International*, Vol 1 (New York, 1977), p98.

2   K Kautsky, *The Erfurt Program* (Chicago, 1910).

3   K Kautsky, *The Road to Power* (Chicago, 1910), p24.

4   See K Kautsky, *Social Revolution*, p45. Also C E Schorske, *German Social Democracy* 1905-1917 (Cambridge, Mass, 1955), p115.

5   K Kautsky, ibid, p47.

6   K Kautsky, *The Erfurt Program*, p188.

7   Ibid.

8   Ibid, p189.

9   K Kautsky, *The Road to Power*, p95.

10 L Trotsky in *Nashe Slovo*, 17 October 1915. Quoted in L Trotsky, *Permanent Revolution* (London, 1962), p254.

11 Eg although these are referred to as 'organs of revolutionary rule', in an important article on perspectives in *Sotsial-Democrat* in 1915, they receive very little emphasis—references to them accounting for only five or six lines in an article of four pages.

12 Cf both *Organisational Questions of the Russian Social Democracy* (published by her epigones under the title *Leninism or Marxism?*), and *The Mass Strike, the Political Party and the Trade Unions* (Bookmarks, London, 1986).

13 R Luxemburg, *Leninism or Marxism?* (Ann Arbor, 1962), p82. Interestingly enough, Lenin, in his reply, does not concentrate on the question of centralism in general, but on factual mistakes and distinctions in Luxemburg's article.

14 R Luxemburg, *The Mass Strike*, p57.

15 Ibid.

16 R Luxemburg, *Leninism or Marxism?* p92.

17 Ibid, p94.

18 Ibid, p93.

19 Ibid, p93.

20 L Trotsky, *Results and Prospects* (1906), in *The Permanent Revolution and Results and Prospects* (London, 1962), p246.

21 Quoted in I Deutscher, *The Prophet Armed* (London, 1954), pp92-93.

22 Ibid.

23 Unfortunately there is no room here to deal with Trotsky's later discussion on these matters.

24 V I Lenin, *Collected Works*, Vol VIII, p104.

25 Ibid, Vol VIII, p564.

26 V I Lenin, *Collected Works*, Vol X, p32.

27 Quoted in R Dunayevskaya, *Marxism and Freedom* (New York, 1958), p182.

28 VI Lenin, *The Collapse of the Second International*, in *Collected Works*. Vol XXI, pp257-8.

29 L Trotsky, *History of the Russian Revolution* (London, 1965), p981.

30 V I Lenin, *Collected Works*, Vol XXVI, pp57-58.

31 V I Lenin, *What is to be Done?* (Moscow, no date), p25.

32   See V I Lenin, *Collected Works*, Vol VII, p263.

33   Ibid Vol VI, p491.

34   Ibid, Vol VII, p265.

35   Ibid, Vol VIII, p157.

36   Ibid, Vol VIII, p155.

37   A Gramsci, *Passato e Presente* (Turin, 1951), p55.

38   A Gramsci, *The Modern Prince and other essays* (London, 1957), p59.

39   Ibid, pp66-67.

40   A Gramsci, *Il Materialismo storico e la filosofia di Benedetto Croce* (Turin, 1948), p38.

41   A Gramsci, *The Modern Prince and other essays*, p67.

42   V I Lenin, *Collected Works*, Vol VII, p117.

43   Ibid, Vol VIII, p145.

44   Ibid, Vol VIII, p196.

45   V I Lenin, *What is to be Done?*, p11.

46   V I Lenin, *Collected Works*, Vol VIII, p154.

47   Ibid, Vol VII, p116.

48   For a naive statement of the opposite view see 'An Open Letter to I.S. Comrades', *Solidarity Special*, September 1968.

49   Some confusion creeps into the argument because of the experience of Russia after 1918. The important point, however, is that it is not the form of the party that produces party as opposed to soviet rule, but the decimation of the working class (see C Harman, 'How the Revolution Was Lost', *International Socialism*, First Series, Vol 30). Cliff makes this point in *Trotsky on substitutionism* (chapter 3 of this volume), but, for some unaccountable reason, also says that in Trotsky's early claims that Lenin's theory of organisation was 'substitutionist', 'one can see his prophetic genius, his capacity for looking ahead, to bring into a unified system every facet of life'.

50   T Cliff, *Rosa Luxemburg* (London, 1959), p54. Here again Cliff's desire to honour a great revolutionary seems to overcome a genuine scientific evaluation.

Towards a revolutionary socialist party

Duncan Hallas

The events of the last 40 years largely isolated the revolutionary socialist tradition from the working classes of the West. The first problem is to reintegrate them. The many partial and localised struggles on wages, conditions, housing, rents, education, health and so on, have to be coordinated and unified into a coherent forward movement based on a strategy for the transformation of society.

In human terms, an organised layer of thousands of workers, by hand and by brain, firmly rooted amongst their fellow workers and with a shared consciousness of the necessity for socialism and the way to achieve it, has to be created. Or rather it has to be recreated. For such a layer existed in the 1920s in Britain and internationally. Its disintegration, initially by Stalinism and then by the complex interactions of Stalinism, fascism and neoreformism, reduced the authentic socialist tradition in the advanced capitalist countries to the status of a fringe belief. As it re-emerges from that status, old disputes take on new life. The nature of the socialist organisation is again an issue.

That an organisation of socialist militants is necessary is common ground on the left, a few anarchist purists apart. But what kind of organisation? One view, widespread amongst newly radicalised students and young workers, is that of the libertarians. In the nature of the case this is something of a blanket term covering a number of distinct tendencies. The essence of what they have in common is hostility to centralised, coordinated activity and profound suspicion of anything smacking of 'leadership'. On this view nothing more than a loose federation of working groups is necessary or desirable. The underlying assumptions are that centralised organisations inevitably undergo bureaucratic degeneration and that the spontaneous activities of working people are the sole and sufficient basis for the achievement of socialism.

The evidence for the first assumption is, on the face of it, impressive. The classic social democratic parties of the early 20th century are a textbook example. It was German social democracy that furnished Robert Michels with the material from which he formulated the 'iron law of oligarchy'. The communist parties, founded in the first place to wrest the politically conscious workers from the influence of conservative social democratic bureaucracies, became in time bureaucratised and authoritarian to a degree previously undreamt of in working-class parties. Moreover, the basic mass organisations, the trade unions, have everywhere become a byword for bureaucratisation and this, apparently, irrespective of the political complexion of their leadership.

From this sort of evidence some libertarians draw the conclusion that a revolutionary socialist party is a contradiction in terms. This is, of course, the traditional anarcho-syndicalist position. More commonly it is conceded that a party may, in favourable circumstances, avoid succumbing to the embraces of the establishment. However, the argument goes, such a party, bureaucratised by definition, inevitably contains within its structure the embryo of a new ruling group and will, if successful, create a new exploitative society. The experience of Stalinist parties in power is advanced as evidence here.

Much of the plausibility of views of this sort derives from their highly abstract and therefore universal character. It would be unfair to equate them with the currently fashionable 'naked apery' but there is certainly some similarity in their psychological appeal. Writers like Morris and Ardrey dispense with the difficult and complicated job of analysing actual societies and actual conflicts in order to deduce from an allegedly unchanging human (or animal) nature the 'inevitability' of this or that. In the same way much libertarian thinking proceeds from very general ideas about the evils of formal organisation to highly specific conclusions without much effort to investigate the actual course of events. Thus Stalinism is seen as the 'inevitable' consequence of Lenin's predilection for a centralised party. A few general notions, a few supposed 'universal truths' which are easily mastered in half an hour, become the substitute for serious theoretical equipment. Since the real world is a very complicated place it is highly reassuring to have at one's disposal the ingredients for an instant social wisdom. Unfortunately it is also highly misleading.

The equation 'centralised organisation equals bureaucracy equals degeneration' is in fact a secularised version of the original sin myth. Like its prototype it leads to profoundly reactionary conclusions. For what is really being implied is that working people are incapable of collective democratic control of their own organisations. Granted that in many cases this has proved to be true; to argue that it is necessarily, inevitably true is to argue that socialism is impossible because democracy, in the literal sense, is impossible.

This is precisely the conclusion that was drawn by the 'neo-Machiavellian' social theorists of the early 20th century and which is deeply embedded in modern academic sociology. It lies at the root of modern social democratic theory, such as it is. Of course, libertarian socialists will have none of this. The essence of their position is rejection of the tired old cliché that there must always be elites and masses, leaders and led, rulers and ruled. Nevertheless the opposite conclusion is implicit in their approach to organisational questions for the simple reason that formal organisations are an essential feature of *any* complex society.

In fact, useful argument about the problems of socialist organisation is impossible at the level of 'universal' generalisations. Organisations do not exist in a vacuum. They are composed of actual people in specific historical situations, attempting to solve real problems with a limited number of options open to them. Failure to take adequate account of these rather obvious considerations vitiates discussion. This is particularly clear in the disputes about the origins of Stalinism.

That Bolshevism was the father of Stalinism is an article of faith with most libertarians. It is also the view of the great majority of social democratic, liberal and conservative writers and, of course, in the purely formal sense that the Stalinist bureaucracy emerged from the Bolshevik Party, it is incontestable. But this does not get us very far. By the same reasoning Jesus Christ was the father of the Spanish Inquisition and Abraham Lincoln the father of United States imperialism, but nobody, one hopes, imagines that statements of this type lead to any useful conclusion. The question is how and why Stalinism emerged and what role, if any, the structure of the Bolshevik Party played in the process.

Daniel Cohn-Bendit's treatment of the matter in his book *Obsolete Communism* is instructive. He sets out to show that, 'far from leading the Russian Revolution forwards, the Bolsheviks were responsible for holding back the struggle of the masses between February and October 1917, and later for turning the revolution into a bureaucratic counter-revolution—in both cases because of the party's very nature, structure and ideology'.

The first point is not relevant here and will be discussed later. The second is developed by means of quotations, suitably selected to establish the calculated malevolence of Lenin and Trotsky. It is shown, correctly, that in 1917 Lenin favoured management of enterprises by elected committees of workers and that in 1918 he came out strongly for one man management, that Trotsky in 1920 called for the militarisation of labour and that the suppression of the Kronstadt revolt in 1921 was an important turning point in the process by which the Russian workers lost power. What is really astonishing about Cohn-Bendit's account of these events is his complete omission of any consideration of the circumstances in which they took place. The ravages of war and civil war, the ruin of Russian industry, the actual disintegration of the Russian working class: all this, apparently, has no bearing on the outcome. True it is conceded in passing that Russia was a backward country and was isolated by the failure of the German Revolution but, we are told, 'these general factors can in no way explain the specific turn it [the revolution] took'.

Now it is usually supposed that there is some sort of connection between the type and level of the production of the necessities of life and the kinds of social organisation that are possible at any stage. No doubt it is very unfortunate that this should be so. Otherwise mankind might have leapt straight from the old stone age to socialism.

If, however, it is conceded that one of the preconditions for socialism is a fairly highly developed industry with a high productivity of labour then some of the 'general factors', so casually dismissed by Cohn-Bendit, assume a certain importance. Russia at the time of the revolution was not just a backward country. By the standards of the developed capitalist countries of the time it was very backward indeed: 80 percent of the total population was still engaged in agriculture; the comparable figure for Britain was 4.5 percent of the workforce. The economist Colin Clark estimated the real income per head per occupied person in Russia in

1913 as 306 units; the comparable figure for Britain was 1,071 units. Indeed on Clark's calculations the figure for Britain as early as 1688, some 370 units, was higher than that for Russia in 1913. All such assessments contain a large margin of error no doubt, but even if the maximum allowance is made for this the prospects for an immediate transition to a non-coercive society in early 20th century Russia were very slender indeed. True, man does not live by bread alone, the cultural heritage is also important. And the cultural heritage of Russia was tsarist barbarism. Not surprisingly there was no tendency whatever in the pre-revolutionary Russian Marxist movement that believed that socialism was on the agenda for an isolated Russia, though this illusion had, it is true, been entertained by the Narodniks.

Yet the economic level of 1913, miserable as it was, represented affluence compared to what was to come. War, revolution, civil war and foreign intervention shattered the productive apparatus. By May 1919 Russian industry was reduced to 10 percent of its normal fuel supply (figures from E H Carr's *The Bolshevik Revolution* (London, 1966) Vol 2). By the end of that year 79 percent of the total railway track mileage was out of action—and this in a huge country where motor transport was practically non-existent. By the end of 1920 the output of all manufactured goods had fallen to 12.9 percent of the 1913 level.

The effect on the working class was catastrophic. As early as December 1918 the number of workers in Petrograd had fallen to half the level of two years earlier. By December 1920 that city had lost 57.5 percent of its total population. In the same three years Moscow lost 44.5 percent.

The number of industrial workers proper was over three million in 1917. In 1921 it had fallen to one and a quarter million. The Russian working class was disappearing into the countryside to avoid literal starvation. And what a countryside! War, famine, typhus, forced requisitioning by red and white alike, the disappearance of even such manufactured goods as matches, paraffin and thread—this was the reality in the Russia of 1920-21. According to Trotsky even cannibalism was reported from several provinces.

In these desperate conditions the Bolshevik Party came to substitute its own rule for that of a decimated, exhausted working class that was itself a small fraction of the population, and within the party the growing apparatus increasingly edged the membership from control. All this is incontestable, but it seems reasonable to suppose that the actual situation had rather more influence on these developments than the 'very nature, structure and ideology' of the party. As a matter of fact the party regime was astonishingly liberal in this period.

The most balanced summary of the matter is that of Victor Serge, himself a communist with strong libertarian leanings, an eye witness and a participant.

> It is often said that 'the germ of all Stalinism was in Bolshevism at its beginning'. Well, I have no objection. Only, Bolshevism also contained many other germs—a mass of other germs—and those who lived through the enthusiasm of the first years of the first victorious revolution ought not to forget it. To judge the living man by the death germs which the autopsy reveals in a corpse—and which he may have carried in him since his birth—is this very sensible?

Given the backwardness of Russia, which germs flourished and which stagnated, which of the several potential outcomes actually materialised, depended above all on the international situation.

The Bolshevik seizure of power took place in the context of a European revolution. The revolutionary movements proved strong enough to over-throw the German Kaiser, the Austrian Emperor and the Turkish Sultan as well as the Russian Tsar. They proved strong enough to prevent a foreign intervention sufficiently massive and sustained to overthrow the Soviet regime, assisted of course by the conflicts between the remaining great powers. But they were aborted or crushed before the critical transi-tion, the establishment of working-class power in one or two advanced countries, was reached. The failure of the German Revolution in 1918-19 to pass beyond the stage of the capitalist democratic republic seems, in retrospect, to have been decisive. The defeat of the Spartacists sealed the fate of working-class rule in Russia, for only substantial economic aid from an advanced economy, in practice from a socialist Germany, could have reversed the disintegration of the Russian working class.

The actual outcome, the transformation of what Lenin, in 1921, called a 'workers' and peasants' state which is bureaucratically deformed' into a totalitarian state capitalism, was itself complex and lengthy. The point that is relevant to this discussion is that an essential part of that process was the destruction of all the wings and tendencies of the Bolshevik Party. It was not sufficient for the counter-revolution to liquidate the various oppositions of left and right. So little was the party suitable as an instrument 'for turning the revolution into a bureaucratic counter-revolution' that most of the original Stalinist cadre too had to be eliminated before the new ruling class stabilised its position.

By 1934, the year of the 17th Party Congress, all open opposition in the party had long been suppressed. The fate of the delegates to that Congress, Stalinists almost to a man, was revealed by Khrushchev in 1956. 'Of the 1,966 delegates, 1,108 were arrested. . . . Of the 139 members and candidates of the party's central committee elected at the Congress 98, ie 70 percent, were arrested and shot.' In short, the vast majority of those who had any roots in the Bolshevik past—80 percent of the 17th Congress delegates had joined by 1921—were liquidated and replaced by new personnel 'uncontaminated' by even the most tenuous ties with the working-class movement.

These events, which have had such profound and lasting consequences, are facts of an altogether different order of magnitude from the deficiencies, real or alleged, of Bolshevik organisational practice. To suppose otherwise is to fall into that extreme voluntarism which many libertarians share with the Maoists.

It does not follow that the last word in organisational wisdom is to be found in the Bolshevik model. In the very different conditions of late 20th century capitalism arguments for or against Lenin's position of 1903 are not so much right or wrong as irrelevant. The 'vanguard partyism' of some of the Maoist and Trotskyist sects is the obverse of the libertarian coin. Both alike are based on a highly abstract and misleading view of reality.

What is in dispute here is in part the usefulness of the analogy. It is clear that any substantial revolutionary socialist party is necessarily, in one sense, a 'vanguard'. But there is no substance in the argument that the concept is elitist. The essence of elitism is the assertion that the observable differences in abilities, consciousness and experience are rooted in unalterable genetic or social conditions and that the mass of the people are incapable of self government now or in the future. Rejection of the elitist position implies that the observed differences are wholly or partly attributable to causes that can be changed. It does not mean denial of the differences themselves.

The real objection to the emphasis on the 'vanguard party' is that it is often part of an obsolete world outlook that directs attention away from contemporary problems and leads, in extreme cases, to a systematic false consciousness, an ideology in the strict Marxian sense of that term.

A vanguard implies a main body, marching in roughly the same direction and imbued with some sort of common outlook and shared aspiration.

When, for example, Trotsky described the German Communist Party of the 20s and early 30s as the vanguard of the German working class, the characterisation was apt. Not only did the party itself include, amongst its quarter of a million or so members, the most enlightened, energetic and self confident of the German workers; it operated in a working class which, in its vast majority, had absorbed some of the basic elements of Marxist thought and which was confronted, especially after 1929, with a deepening social crisis which could not be resolved within the framework of the Weimar Republic.

In that situation the actions of the party were of decisive importance. What it did, or failed to do, influenced the whole subsequent course of European and world history. The sharp polemics about the details of tactics, history and theory, which were the staple output of the oppositional communist groups of the period, were entirely justified and necessary. In the given circumstances the vanguard *was* decisive. In Trotsky's striking metaphor, switching the points could change the direction of the whole heavy train of the German workers' movement.

Today the circumstances are quite different. There is no train. A new generation of capable and energetic workers exists but they are no longer part of a cohesive movement and they no longer work in a milieu where basic Marxist ideas are widespread. We are back at our starting point. Not only has the vanguard, in the real sense of a considerable layer of organised revolutionary workers and intellectuals, been destroyed. So too has the environment, the tradition, that gave it influence. In Britain that tradition was never so extensive and influential as in Germany or France but it was real enough in the early years of the Communist Party.

The crux of the matter is how to develop the process, now begun, of recreating it. It may be true, as Gramsci said, that it is harder to create generals than to create an army. It is certainly true that generals without an army are entirely useless; even if it is supposed that they can be created in a vacuum. In fact, 'vanguardism', in its extreme forms, is an idealist perversion of Marxism, which leads to a moralistic view of the class struggle. Workers are seen as straining at the leash, always ready

and eager to fight but always betrayed by corrupt and reactionary leaders. Especially pernicious are the 'left' leaders whose radical phraseology
conceals a fixed determination to sell the pass at the first opportunity.

Such things certainly happen of course. Corruption in the literal
sense is not unknown in the British labour movement and in its more
subtle manifestations it is widespread. But it is grotesquely one sided to
suppose that, for example, the history of Britain since the war can be
explained in terms of 'betrayals' and it is idiotic to imagine that all that
is necessary is to 'build a new leadership' around some sect or other and
then offer it as an alternative to the waiting workers.

The reality is much more complex. The elements of a working-class
leadership already exist. The activists and militants who actually maintain
the shop floor and working-class organisations from day to day are the
leadership in practical terms. That they are, typically, more or less under
the influence of reformist or Stalinist ideas, or ideas more reactionary
still, is not to be explained in terms of betrayal. It is to be explained both
in terms of their own experience and in terms of the absence of a socialist tendency seen as credible and realistic.

The first point has been crucial. Reformist policies have been successful in the advanced economies in the last 20-odd years. Not always
or for everyone but for enough people enough of the time to create a
widespread belief in reformism as a viable proposition.

As conditions change the second point becomes increasingly important and excessive emphasis on the vanguard concept can become a real
barrier to the process of fusing the tradition and the activists.

One of the negative features of the leadership/betrayal syndrome is
the assumption that the answers to all problems are known in advance.
They are contained in a programme which is definitive and final. To
safeguard the purity of the programme is seen as one of the main tasks
of the selected few. That there may be new problems which require
new solutions, that it is necessary to learn from one's fellow workers as
well as to teach, are unwelcome ideas. And yet they are fundamental.
Omniscience is no more granted to organisations than to individuals. A
certain amount of modesty, of flexibility, of awareness of limitations is
necessary.

It is, on the face of it, rather unlikely that a programme written in, let
us say, 1938 contains the complete solution to the questions of the 1970s.
It is certainly the case that in the process of recreating a considerable

socialist movement many old concepts will have to be modified. Ideas, at least useful, operative ideas, have some sort of relationship to facts and it is a platitude that the world in which we work is changing at an unparalleled rate.

As a matter of fact the development of a programme, in the sense of a detailed statement of partial and transitional aims and tactics in all important fields, is inseparable from the development of the movement itself. It presupposes the participation of a large number of people who are themselves actively engaged in those fields. The job of socialists is to connect their theory and aims with the problems and experiences of militants in such a way as to achieve a synthesis that is both a practical guide to action and a springboard for further advance. Such a synthesis is meaningful to the extent that it actually guides the activities of participants and is modified in the light of practice and that changes in circumstances which it itself produces. This is the real meaning of the 'struggle for a programme' that is so often turned into a fetish.

Similar considerations apply to internationalism. Internationalism, the recognition of the long run common interests of workers everywhere and of the priority of this interest over all sectional and national considerations, is basic to socialism. Today, with the increasing weight and influence of great international big business concerns, this is more obvious than ever. There cannot be a purely nationally based socialist organisation. It is one of the merits of the Trotskyist groupings to have consistently emphasised this fundamental truth.

Yet the conclusion often drawn from it—'one must start with the International' is another example of the distorting influence of over-concentration on 'leadership'. An 'International' which consists of no more than a grouping of sects in various countries is a fiction. It is a harmful fiction because, as experience has shown, it leads to delusions of grandeur and hence to evasion of the real problems. The ludicrous situation in which no less than three bodies exist, each claiming to be *the* Fourth International and exchanging mutual anathemas like rival medieval popes, is a sufficient indication of the bankruptcy of ultra-vanguardism in the international field.

To develop a real current of internationalism—and without such a current all talk of an International is self deception—it is necessary to start by linking the concrete struggles of workers in one country with those of others; of Ford workers in Britain and Germany for example, of dockers in London and Rotterdam and so on. This means starting where such workers actually exist, namely in the various countries. It means putting aside grandiose ideas of 'international leadership', 'World Congresses' and the like, in favour of the humdrum tasks of propaganda and agitation in one's own country together with the development of international links which, however limited at first, are meaningful to advanced workers outside the sectarian milieu.

Meetings and discussions between socialist grouplets in the various countries are essential, theoretical discussion is essential but above all the creation of real links between groups of workers is essential. Only after this has been done on a considerable scale will the preconditions for the recreation of the International be achieved. In the existing situation the analogy of Marx and the First International is in some ways more relevant than that of Lenin and the Third. Neither provides a blueprint that can be followed mechanically.

Of course, after all the dross is discarded, there is an important grain of truth in the 'vanguard' analogy. It lies in the recognition of the extreme unevenness of the working people in consciousness, confidence, experience and activity. A rather small and constantly changing fraction of the working class is actually involved, to any extent, in the activities of the existing mass organisations. A larger fraction is episodically involved and the vast majority are drawn into activity only in exceptional circumstances. Moreover, even when largish numbers of workers are engaged in actions—in strikes or rent struggles, etc—these actions are typically sectional and limited in their objectives. The only major exception which occurs more or less regularly, the act of voting for a party seen as, in some sense, the party of the working class is itself increasingly ritualistic in character. And even at this level it has to be remembered that at every election since the war something like one third of the working class has voted Tory.

To state these well known facts is sometimes regarded as something of a betrayal, a slander against the working class. And yet it is merely a statement, not only of what exists, but also of what must exist for capitalist class society in its 'democratic' form to continue at all. Once large numbers of people actually act directly, collectively and continuously to change their conditions they not only change themselves; they undermine the whole basis of capitalism. The relevance of a party is, firstly, that it can give the real vanguard, the more advanced and conscious minority of workers and not the sects or self proclaimed leaders, the confidence and the cohesion necessary to carry the mass with them. It follows that there can be no talk of a party that does not include this minority as one of its major components.

The problem of apathy has to be seen in this context. As has often been pointed out, the essence of apathy is the feeling of powerlessness, of inability to change the course of events in more than a marginal way, if that. The growth of apathy, the increase in atomisation, in turning one's back on the world, is naturally closely connected with the decline in the ability of reformist politics to deliver the goods as the power of the international capitalist firms to evade 'national' restrictions grows steadily. This is why apathy can be very rapidly turned into its opposite if a credible alternative is presented.

That alternative must be more than a mere collection of individuals giving general adherence to a platform. It must also be a centre for mutual training and debate, for raising the level of the raw activist to that of the experienced, for the fusion of the experiences and outlook of manual and white collar workers and intellectuals with ideas of scientific socialism. It must be a substitute for those institutions, special schools, universities, clubs, messes and so on, through which the ruling class imbues its cadres with a common outlook, tradition and loyalty. And it must do this without cutting off its militants from their fellow workers.

That hoary red herring, the question of whether socialist consciousness arises 'spontaneously' amongst workers or is imposed by intellectuals from the 'outside' has absolutely no relevance to modern conditions. It is strictly a non-question because it assumes the existence of a more or less autonomous working-class world outlook into which something is injected. Whether the relatively homogeneous working-class outlook, so lovingly described by writers like Richard Hoggart, was ever so autonomous as has often been supposed may be questioned. In any case it is dead, killed by changing social conditions and above all by the mass media. It is rather ridiculous to argue about whether one should bring ideas from 'outside' to workers who own television sets. Certainly most workers and especially the activists see things rather differently than the denizens of the stockbroker belt. Their whole life experience ensures this. But workers are not automata responding passively to the environment. Everyone has to have some picture of the world, some frame of reference into which data are fitted, some assumptions about society.

The whole vast apparatus of mass communications, educational institutions and the rest have, as one of their principal functions, what sociologists call 'socialisation' and what the old Wobblies called head fixing. The assumptions convenient to the ruling class are the daily diet of all of us. Individuals, whether bus drivers or lecturers in aesthetics, can resist the conditioning process to a point. Only a collective can develop a systematic alternative world view, can overcome to some degree the alienation of manual and mental work that imposes on everyone, on workers and intellectuals alike, a partial and fragmented view of reality. What Rosa Luxemburg called 'the fusion of science and the workers' is unthinkable outside a revolutionary party.

Such a party cannot possibly be created except on a thoroughly democratic basis; unless, in its internal life, vigorous controversy is the rule and various tendencies and shades of opinion are represented, a socialist party cannot rise above the level of a sect. Internal democracy is not an optional extra. It is fundamental to the relationship between party members and those amongst whom they work.

The point was well illustrated by Isaac Deutscher in discussing the communist parties in the late 20s and early 30s.

> When the European communist went out to argue his case before a working-class audience, he usually met there a social democratic opponent whose arguments he had to refute and whose slogans he had to counter. Most frequently he was unable to do this, because he lacked the habits of political debate, which were not cultivated within the party, and because his schooling deprived him of the ability to preach to the unconverted. He could not probe adequately into his opponents' case when he had to think all the time about his own orthodoxy... He could propound with mechanical fanaticism a prescribed set of arguments and slogans... When called upon, as he often was, to answer criticism of the Soviet Union, he could rarely do so convincingly, his thanksgiving prayers to the workers' fatherland and his hosannahs for Stalin covered him with ridicule in the eyes of any sober-minded audience. This ineffectiveness of the Stalinist agitation was one of the main reasons why over many years, even in the most favourable circumstances, that agitation made little or no headway against social democratic reformism.

Latter day parallels will spring to mind.

The self education of militants is impossible in an atmosphere of sterile orthodoxy. Self reliance and confidence in one's ideas are developed in the course of that genuine debate that takes place in an atmosphere where differences are freely and openly argued. The 'monolithic party' is a Stalinist concept. Uniformity and democracy are mutually incompatible.

Naturally a party cannot be a holdall in which any and every conceivable standpoint is represented. The limits of membership are determined by a serious commitment to the ultimate objective: the democratic collective control by the working class over industry and society. Within these limits a variety of views on aspects of strategy and tactics is necessary and inevitable in a democratic organisation. The heresy hunting characteristic of certain sects is self defeating; an atmosphere of quasi-religious fanaticism is incompatible with the reintegration of the socialist tradition with a broad layer of workers.

The discipline that is certainly necessary in any serious organisation can arise in one of two ways. It can arise from a system of artificial unanimity enforced by edicts and prescriptions, a system that is counterproductive in a socialist group. Or it can arise from a common tradition and loyalty built on the basis of common work, mutual education and a realistic and responsible relationship to the spontaneous activities of workers.

Spontaneity is a fact. But what does it mean? Simply that groups of workers who are not active with any political or even trade union organisation take action on their own behalf or in support of others. From the point of view of organisations the action is 'spontaneous'; from the point of view of the workers concerned it is conscious and deliberate. Such activity is constantly occurring and reflects the aspirations for self government that are widespread even amongst workers commonly regarded as 'backward'. It is an elemental expression of the class struggle. Without it conscious militants would be suspended in a vacuum. To use the hackneyed but useful analogy, it is the steam that drives the pistons of working-class organisation.

Pistons without propellants are useless. Steam unchannelled has only a limited effect. Spontaneity and organisation are not alternatives; they are different aspects of the process by which increasing numbers of workers can become conscious of the reality of their situation and of their power to change it. The growth of that process depends on a dialogue, on organised militants who listen as well as argue, who understand the limitations of a party as well as its strengths and who are able to find connections between the actual consciousness of their fellows and the politics necessary to realise the aspirations buried in that consciousness.

It sometimes happens that even the best militants find themselves overtaken by events and occupying a position, for a shorter or longer time, to the right of previously unmilitant workers. The experience is familiar to active rank-and-file trade unionists. Slogans and demands that were yesterday acceptable only to the more conscious people can quite suddenly be too limited for the majority when a struggle develops beyond the expected point. Inevitably the greater experience and knowledge of the activists induces a certain caution, normally appropriate, but which, in a rapidly changing situation, can sometimes become a real barrier to advance. The same tendency is bound to occur with an organisation. This is the valid element in Cohn-Bendit's critique of socialist parties.

The danger is inherent in the nature of the environment. Sudden changes of consciousness amongst this group or that cannot always or even usually be predicted. What can be predicted is the need for the sensitivity to detect them rapidly and the flexibility to react appropriately.

Neither the existence of such spontaneous changes of mood, unexpected upheavals nor the frequent tendency towards caution amongst the layer of experienced and committed socialists constitute an argument against a party. On the contrary, given the unevenness of consciousness and the industrial and geographical divisions of the working class, a party, indeed a centralised party, is essential to give to various actions of different groups that cohesion and coordination without which their effect will be limited to local and sectional gains.

It is an argument against that bureaucratic caricature of a party that Stalinism has caused many on the left to confuse with the genuine article. One of Cohn-Bendit's chosen illustrations of party conservatism, the fact that in July 1917 the Bolshevik Party lagged behind the workers of Petrograd and tried to restrain and limit their demonstrations, illuminates the point. The party was caught in a dilemma inherent in the uneven development of the movement in Russia as a whole. As Trotsky wrote 'there was the fear that Petrograd might become isolated from the more backward provinces; on the other hand there was the hope that an active and energetic intervention by Petrograd might save the situation'. This 'conservatism' was a reflection of the pressure of the party members in other centres who, in turn, transmitted the mood of working-class circles in these centres. The fact that there was a party sufficiently flexible to react to that pressure probably prevented a repetition of the Paris Commune in 1917. This, of course, was the most extreme situation possible but similar problems are inevitable at every stage of development.

A revolutionary socialist party is necessary then; but such a party has been necessary for a long time. Why should it be supposed that it is possible to create it in the 1970s?

Basically the case rests on the analysis of the world crisis developed in *International Socialism*, and particularly on the thesis that, in the changing conditions of capitalism, reformist policies will be less and less able to provide those partial solutions to the problems confronting the working class that they have been able to provide in the decades since the Second World War. This is the objective factor.

The most important subjective factor is the decline in the ideological power of Stalinism. The past influence of Stalinism on the left and its effects, direct and by reaction, in effectively excluding the building of an alternative are difficult to exaggerate. For 15 years that power has been eroded, slowly at first and then more and more quickly. Today it is in full disintegration. This ideological decomposition is not to be confused with the organisational decline of communist parties. Though the British party has certainly declined this is not the decisive consideration. The party still commands the allegiance of a good many industrial militants. But it no longer commands it on the old basis. It is no longer a Stalinist party. All kinds of tendencies exist within it and now that the papal infallibility of Moscow is gone for ever the monolithic party cannot be restored.

The dominant group in the party, the Gollan leadership, is effectively reformist. Whether, as some of its critics suspect, the leadership aims to liquidate the party into the Labour Party, or whether, as seems more likely, it clings to the illusion that there is room in British politics for a second reformist workers' party, makes little difference. As an obstacle to regroupment on the left the party is a rapidly waning force.

Nor is the Labour Party left the force it used to be. In part this is a reflection of the decline of the Communist Party, for every significant left wing in the Labour Party in the past has leaned heavily on the Communist Party's trade union base. In part it is an effect of the decline of the Labour Party's own membership organisations—youth, wards, constituencies—which has become so marked in recent years. There are still genuine socialists active in the Labour Party as there are also amongst the passive cardholders. But it seems unlikely, though it is not inconceivable, that any fairly massive socialist current will develop in the party.

The basis for the beginnings of a revolutionary socialist party exists amongst those industrial militants who used to look to the Communist Party, amongst increasing numbers of radicalised young workers and students and amongst the revolutionary groups.

The latter are an important but difficult problem. The root cause of the sort of sectarianism that has plagued the British left is the isolation of socialists from effective and influential participation in mass struggles. The isolation is rapidly diminishing but its negative effects—the exacerbation of secondary differences, the transformation of tactical differences into matters of principle, the semireligious fanaticism which can give a group considerable survival power in adverse conditions at the cost of stunting its potentiality for real development, the theoretical conservatism and blindness to unwelcome aspects of reality—all these persist. They will be overcome when, and only when, a serious penetration and fusion of layers of workers and students outside sectarian circles has been achieved. The International Socialists [forerunner to the Socialist Workers Party—editor] intend to make a significant contribution to that penetration. Without having any illusions that it is 'the leadership' the group exists to make a theoretical and a practical contribution to the regeneration of socialism in Britain and internationally.

Trotsky on substitutionism

Tony Cliff

Twenty years ago Trotsky was assassinated. The best tribute one can pay to this great revolutionary, who so despised all cant, would be a critical study of some of his ideas. We offer the following study of one problem he so brilliantly posed as a very young man, a problem that plagued him for the rest of his life, and that is still with us: the problem of the relation between party and class and the danger of the former substituting for the latter.

Quite early in his political activity, when only 24 years old, Trotsky prophesied that Lenin's conception of party organisation must lead to a situation in which the party would '*substitute* itself for the working classes', act as proxy in their name and on their behalf, regardless of what the workers thought or wanted.

Lenin's conception would lead to a state of affairs in which 'the organisation of the party substitutes itself for the party as a whole; then the central committee substitutes itself for the organisation; and finally the "dictator" substitutes himself for the central committee.'[1]

To Lenin's type of centralised party made up of professional revolutionaries, Trotsky counterposed a 'broadly based party' on the model of the Western European social democratic parties. He saw the only guarantee against 'substitutionism'—the term he coined—in the mass party, democratically run and under the control of the proletarian masses.

He wound up his argument with the following plea against uniformity:

The tasks of the new regime will be so complex that they cannot be solved otherwise than by way of competition between various methods of economic and political construction, by way of long 'disputes', by way of a systematic struggle not only between the socialist and capitalist worlds, but also many trends inside socialism, trends which will inevitably emerge as soon as the proletarian dictatorship poses tens and hundreds of new... problems. No strong 'domineering' organisation...will be able to suppress these trends and controversies... A proletariat capable of exercising its dictatorship over society will not tolerate any dictatorship over itself...

The working class...will undoubtedly have in its ranks quite a few political invalids...and much ballast of obsolescent ideas, which it will have to jettison. In the epoch of its dictatorship, as now, it will have to cleanse its mind of false theories and bourgeois experience and to purge its ranks of political phrasemongers and backward-looking revolutionaries... But this intricate task cannot be solved by placing above the proletariat a few well picked people...or one person invested with the power to liquidate and degrade.[2]

In Trotsky's words about the danger of 'substitutionism' inherent in Lenin's conception of party organisation, and his plea against uniformity, one can see his prophetic genius, his capacity to look ahead, to bring into a unified system every facet of life.

The history of Bolshevism since 1917 seems to have completely vindicated Trotsky's warning of 1904. But Trotsky never returned to it again. In the present article we shall try to find out why he did not, to reveal the roots of 'substitutionism' in particular and to look at the problem of the relation between the party and the class in general.

The problem of substitutionism

'Substitutionism' is in the tradition of the Russian revolutionary movement. In the sixties and seventies of the 19th century, small groups, mere handfuls, of intellectuals, pitted themselves against the mighty autocracy, while the mass of peasants in whose name and interests these heroic Narodniks (Populists) acted remained indifferent, or even hostile to them.

In the morass of general apathy, before a mass movement of any kind appeared, these mere handfuls of rebellious intellectuals played an important, progressive role. Marx was not the least to accord them the greatest praise and admiration. Thus for instance, he wrote to his eldest daughter, in the very year in which the People's Will was crushed:

These are admirable men, without any melodramatic pose, full of simplicity, real heroes. Making an outcry and taking action are two things completely opposite which cannot be reconciled.

'Substitutionism', however, becomes a reactionary, dangerous element when a rising mass movement already exists and the party tries to substitute itself for this. Trotsky was too scientific a thinker to believe that in the conception, right or wrong, of the party and its role and relations with the class, one can find sufficient guarantee against 'substitutionism' and for real democracy in the workers' political movement.

The objective conditions necessary to avoid it were clearly formulated by Trotsky a few months before he wrote the above quoted work, when he said at the Second Congress of the Russian Social Democratic Workers Party (RSDLP) in London in 1903:

> The rule of the working class was inconceivable until the great mass of them were united in desiring it. Then they would be an overwhelming majority. This would not be the dictatorship of a little band of conspirators or a minority party, but of the immense majority in the interests of the immense majority, to prevent counter-revolution. In short, it would represent the victory of true democracy.

This paraphrase of the *Communist Manifesto* is absolutely in harmony with Trotsky's struggle against 'substitutionism'. If the majority rules, there is no place for a minority to act as its proxy.

During the same period Lenin was not less emphatic in saying that any dictatorship of the proletariat when this was a small minority in society must lead to anti-democratic and, in his words, 'reactionary conclusions'.

When Trotsky, putting aside his own words, called for a workers' government as an immediate aim of the revolutionary movement in Russia, Lenin answered sharply:

> That cannot be! It cannot be because a revolutionary dictatorship can endure for a time only if it rests on the enormous majority of the people... The proletariat constitutes a minority... Anyone who attempts to achieve socialism by any other route without passing through the stage of political democracy, will inevitably arrive at the most absurd and reactionary conclusions, both economic and political.[3]

Trotsky's warning against 'substitutionism' and his emphasis on the rule of 'the immense majority in the interests of the immense majority' as the only guarantee against it is indeed a crying contradiction to his call for a workers' government in 1905 and 1917, when the workers were a tiny minority. Trotsky is torn in the contradiction between his consistent, socialist, democratic conception of opposition to any form of 'substitutionism' and his theory of the Permanent Revolution, in which the proletarian minority acts as a proxy for all the toilers, and as the ruler of society. Alas, this contradiction is not the result of any failure in Trotsky's thinking, of any inconsistency, but is a reflection of actual contradictions in the objective conditions.

The nature of the revolution, including its actual timing, are not dependent on the size of the working class alone and not even on its level of class consciousness and organisation, but on many mixed and contradictory factors. The factors leading to revolution—economic stresses, wars or other political and social upheavals—are not synchronised with the enlightenment of the proletariat. A whole number of objective circumstances impel the workers to revolution, while the unevenness in consciousness of different sections and groups in the working class can be quite marked. In a backward country, as Tsarist Russia was, where the workers' general cultural level was low, and traditions of organisation and mass self activity weak, this unevenness was particularly marked. And there the working class as a whole was such a small minority that its rule, the dictatorship of the proletariat, had to be the dictatorship not of the majority but of a tiny minority.

To overcome the actual dilemma facing the revolution in Russia—to avoid minority rule on the one hand, and to avoid the passive abstentionist attitude of the Mensheviks ('the proletariat should not take power so long as it is a minority in society')—Trotsky looked to two main factors: the revolutionary impulse and activity of the Russian workers, and the spread of the revolution to more advanced countries where the proletariat made up the majority of society.

However, what was the fate of 'substitutionism' with the decline of the revolutionary impulse in Russia itself, and, not less decisive, with the breaking of the revolutionary struggles in the West on the rocks of capitalism?

Substitutionism in Russia

While the relation between the party and the class was affected by the level of culture and revolutionary consciousness of the working class, it was also influenced by the specific weight of the working class in society: by the size of the class and its relations with other classes, above all—in Russia—with the peasantry.

Now, if the Russian Revolution was a simon-pure bourgeois revolution (as the Mensheviks argued) or if it was a simon-pure socialist one (as the anarchists and Social Revolutionaries who did not distinguish between workers and peasants argued) the question would have been simple. A relative social homogeneity of the revolutionary classes would have constituted a large enough anvil on which to batter out of existence any trend towards the Marxist party substituting for the proletariat.

However, the October Revolution was the fusion of two revolutions: that of the socialist working class, the product of mature capitalism, and that of the peasants, the product of the conflict between rising capitalism and the old feudal institutions. As at all times, the peasants were ready enough to expropriate the private property of the large estate owners, but they wanted their own small *private* properties. Whilst they were prepared to revolt against feudalism, they were not for that reason in favour of socialism.

Hence it is not surprising that the victorious alliance of workers and peasants in the October Revolution was immediately followed by very strained relations. Once the White armies, and with them the danger of the restoration of landlordism, had been overcome, very little remained of the peasants' loyalty towards the workers. It had been one thing for the peasant to support a government which distributed land, but it was quite another matter when the same government began to requisition his produce to feed the hungry populations in the cities.

The conflict between the working class and the peasantry was expressed from the beginning of the October Revolution in the fact that already in 1918 Lenin was compelled to take refuge in the anti-democratic measure of counting one worker's vote as equal to five peasants' in the elections to the soviets.

Now the revolution itself changed the relative weight of the proletariat vis à vis that of the peasantry, to the detriment of the former.

First, the civil war led to a terrible decline in the specific weight of the working class. The working-class victory in the revolution led paradoxically to a decline in the size and quality of the working class.

As many of the urban workers had close connections with the villages, considerable numbers of them hurried back to the countryside as soon as the revolution was over, in order to share in the land distribution. This tendency was further encouraged by the food shortage from which, naturally, the towns suffered the most. Moreover, in sharp contrast to the old Tsarist army, the new Red Army included relatively more industrial workers than peasants. For all these reasons the town population, and particularly the numbers of industrial workers, declined very sharply between 1917 and 1920. The population of Petrograd fell by 57.5 percent, of Moscow by 44.5 percent, of 40 provincial capitals by 33 percent, and of another 50 large towns by 16 percent. The larger the city the greater was the relative loss in population. How sharp was the decline is further illustrated by the fact that the number of workers in industry fell from 3,000,000 in 1917 to 1,240,000 in 1921-22, a decrease of 58.7 percent. The number of industrial workers thus declined by three fifths. And the productivity of these workers declined even more than their number. (In 1920, the industrial production of Russia was only some 13 percent of that of 1913!)

Of those remaining the big majority were the most backward workers who were not needed for the different military fronts or for the administration of the state, trade unions and party. The state administration and army naturally drew most of their recruits from that section of the workers with the oldest socialist tradition, the greatest political experience and highest culture.

The fragmentation of the working class had an even worse effect. The remainder of the working class was forced by the scarcity of food to behave rather as small individualist traders than as a collective, as a united class. It has been calculated that in 1919-20 the state supplied only 42 percent of the grain consumed by the towns, and an even smaller percentage of other foodstuffs, all the rest being bought on the black market.[4] The sale by workers of furniture and clothing, and also belts and tools from factories where they worked, was quite common.[5] What an atomisation and demoralisation of the industrial working class!

In their mode of living—relying on individual illicit trade—the individual workers were hardly distinguishable from the peasants. As

Rudzutak put it to the Second Congress of Trade Unions in January 1919:

> We observe in a large number of industrial centres that the workers, thanks to the contraction of production in the factories, are being absorbed in the peasant mass, and instead of a population of workers we are getting a half peasant or sometimes a purely peasant population.[6]

Under such conditions the class base of the Bolshevik Party disintegrated—not because of some mistakes in the policies of Bolshevism, not because of one or another conception of Bolshevism regarding the role of the party and its relation to the class—but because of mightier historical factors. The working class had become declassed.

It is true that in despair, or in desperation, Lenin could say in May 1921: 'Even when the proletariat has to live through a period of being declassed, it can still carry out its task of conquering and retaining power.'[7] But what an extremely 'substitutionist' formulation this is. Declassed working-class rule—the Cheshire cat's smile after the cat has disappeared.

In the case of the Narodniks, the 'substitutionist' conception was not a primary cause, but a result of the general apathy and stupor of the people which in turn was rooted in objective social conditions. Now again, in the case of Bolshevik 'substitutionism', it did not jump out of Lenin's head as Minerva out of Zeus's, but was born of the objective conditions of civil war in a peasant country, where a small working class, reduced in weight, became fragmented and dissolved into the peasant masses.

An analogy might help to clarify the rise of 'substitutionism' after the October Revolution. One must only imagine a mass strike in which, after a prolonged period, the majority of the workers become tired and demoralised with only a minority continuing to picket, attacked by the boss and derided and resented by the majority of workers. This tragic situation is repeated again and again on the battleground of the class struggle. In the face of the White Guard, with the knowledge that a terrible bloodbath threatened the people if the Bolsheviks gave up the struggle and with the knowledge of their own isolation, the Bolsheviks did not find a way out. 'Substitutionism', like all fetishisms, was a reflection of social impasse.

Substitutionism in the party

From here it is a short step to the abolition of inner party democracy, and the establishment of the rule of officialdom within it.

Contrary to Stalinist mythology—as well as that of the Mensheviks and other opponents of the Bolsheviks—the Bolshevik Party had never been a monolithic or totalitarian party. Far from it. Internal democracy had always been of the utmost importance in party life, but for one reason or another, this has been glossed over in most of the literature dealing with the subject. It is therefore worthwhile to digress somewhat and devote a little space to setting out a number of cases which illustrate the degree of inner party democracy and the lack of monolithism in the history of Bolshevism.

In 1907, after the final defeat of the revolution, the party suffered a crisis over the question of what attitude to take to the elections to the Tsarist Duma. At the Third Conference of the Russian Social Democratic Workers Party (held in July 1907), in which Bolsheviks as well as Mensheviks were represented, a curious situation arose: all the Bolshevik delegates, with the sole exception of Lenin, voted in favour of boycotting the elections to the Duma; Lenin voted with the Mensheviks.[8] Three years later a plenum of the Central Committee of the Bolsheviks passed a resolution calling for unity with the Mensheviks; again the only dissentient voice was Lenin's.[9]

When the 1914-18 war broke out, not one of the party's branches adopted the revolutionary defeatist position which Lenin advocated,[10] and at a trial of some Bolshevik leaders in 1915 Kamenev and two Bolshevik Duma deputies publicly repudiated Lenin's revolutionary defeatist position in court.[11]

After the February Revolution the large majority of the party leaders were not for a revolutionary soviet government, but for support of the coalition provisional government. The Bolshevik faction had 40 members in the Petrograd Soviet on 2 March, 1917, but when the resolution to transfer power to the bourgeois coalition government was put to the vote, only 19 voted against.[12] At a meeting of the Petrograd Committee of the Party (5 March, 1917), a resolution for a revolutionary soviet government received only one vote.[13] *Pravda*, edited by Stalin at that time, had a position which can in no way be called revolutionary. It decisively declared its support for the provisional government 'insofar as it struggles against reaction or counter-revolution'.[14]

Again, when Lenin came to Russia on 3rd April, 1917, and issued his famous 'April Theses'—a light guiding the party to the October Revolution—he was for a time in a small minority in his own party. *Pravda's* comment on the 'April Theses' was that it was 'Lenin's personal opinion', and quite 'unacceptable'.[15] At a meeting of the Petrograd Committee of the party, held on 8 April, 1917, the 'Theses' received only two votes, while 13 voted against and one abstained.[16] However, at the conference of the party held 14-22 April, the 'Theses' gained a majority: 71 for, 39 against and eight abstentions.[17] The same conference defeated Lenin on another important question, namely whether the party should participate in the proposed Stockholm conference of the socialist parties. Against his views, it decided in favour of full participation.[18]

Again, on 14 September Kerensky convened a 'Democratic Conference' and Lenin spoke strongly in favour of boycotting it. The Central Committee supported him by nine votes to eight, but as the vote was so nearly equal, the final decision was left to the party conference, which was to be constituted out of the Bolshevik faction in the 'Democratic Conference'. This meeting decided by 77 votes to 50 not to boycott it.[19]

When the most important question of all, the question of the October insurrection, was the order of the day, the leadership again was found to be sharply divided: a strong faction, led by Zinoviev, Kamenev, Rykov, Piatamov, Miliutin and Nogin, opposed the uprising. Nevertheless, when the Political Bureau was elected by the Central Committee, neither Zinoviev nor Kamenev were excluded.

After taking power, the differences in the party leadership continued to be as sharp as before. A few days after the revolution, a number of party leaders came out with a demand for a coalition with other socialist parties. Those insisting on this included Rykov, the People's Commissar of the Interior, Miliutin, the People's Commissar of Industry and Trade, Lunacharsky, the Commissar of Labour, Kamenev, the President of the Republic, and Zinoviev. They went as far as resigning from the government, thus compelling Lenin and his supporters to open negotiations with the other parties. (The negotiations broke down because the Mensheviks insisted on the exclusion of Lenin and Trotsky from the coalition government.)

Again, on the question of holding or postponing the elections to the Constituent Assembly (in December 1917), Lenin found himself in a minority in the Central Committee, and the elections were held against his advice.[20] A little later he was again defeated on the question of the peace negotiations with Germany at Brest-Litovsk. He was for an immediate peace. But at a meeting of the Central Committee and active workers, held on 21 January 1918, his motion received only 15 votes against Bukharin's motion for 'revolutionary war', which received 32 votes, and Trotsky's, for 'neither peace nor war', which received 16.[21] At a session of the Central Committee the next day, Lenin was again defeated. But at last he succeeded, under the pressure of events, in convincing the majority of members of the Central Committee of his point of view, and at its session on 24 February his motion for peace gained seven votes, while four voted against and another four abstained.[22]

However, inner party democracy dwindled under the pressure of the objective circumstances referred to above. Isolated, the party became frightened to think aloud, to voice disagreements. It was as if they were in a small rickety boat in the midst of rapids. The atmosphere of free discussion necessarily died.

The breaches of inner party democracy became worse and worse. Thus K K Yurenev, for example, spoke at the Ninth Congress (April 1920) of the methods used by the Central Committee to suppress criticism, including the virtual exile of the critics: 'One goes to Christiana, another sent to the Urals, a third—to Siberia.'[23] He said that, in its attitude towards the party, the Central Committee had become 'not accountable ministry, but unaccountable government'. At the same congress, V N Maximovsky counterposed 'democratic centralism' to the 'bureaucratic centralism' for which the centre was responsible. 'It is said', he commented, 'that fish begin to rot from the head. The party begins to suffer at the top from the influence of bureaucratic centralism.'[24] And Sapranov declared: 'However much you talk about electoral rights, about the dictatorship of the proletariat, or the yearning of the Central Committee for the party dictatorship, in fact this leads to the dictatorship of the party bureaucracy.'[25]

At the Eleventh Congress, Riazanov said:

> Our Central Committee is altogether a special institution. It is said that the English parliament is omnipotent: it is only unable to change a man into a woman. Our Central Committee is more powerful: it has already changed more than one very revolutionary man into an old lady and the number of these old ladies has increased incredibly.[26]

He further accused it of intervening in all aspects of party life. V Kosior gave many examples of local leaders both of the party and of the trade unions being removed by decisions of the Political Bureau or the Orgbureau:

> Many workers are leaving the party. How to explain this? This, dear comrades, is to be explained by the strong hand regime, which has nothing in common with real party discipline and which is cultivated among us. Our party carries wood, sweeps the streets and even votes, but decides no questions. But the not very healthy proletariat finds itself in these surroundings, and cannot stand it.[27]

At the Twelfth Congress, Preobrazhensky complained that 30 percent of the secretaries of the gubernia party committees were 'recommended' for the positions by the Central Committee of the party, thus violating the principle of election of all party officials.[28] From here it was but a step to the supreme rule of the general secretary.

One can say without hesitation that the substitution of a ruling working class for a capitalist class—where capitalism was in its infancy and where the majority of the people were small capitalists (peasants)—was the cause of the substitution of the Marxist party for the working class, and that this led to the substitution of the officialdom for the party, and finally to the individual dictatorship of the general secretary.

Marx and Engels dealt more than once with the question of what would happen if the working class took power before the historical prerequisites for the substitution of capitalist relations of production by socialist ones were present. They concluded that in such an event the working class would blaze a path for developing capitalism. Engels wrote:

> The worst thing that can befall a leader of an extreme party is to be compelled to take over a government in an epoch when the movement is not yet ripe for the domination of the class which he represents and for the realisation of the measures which that domination would imply... he necessarily finds himself in a dilemma. What he *can* do is in contrast to all his actions as hitherto practised, to all his principles and to the present interests of his party; what he *ought* to do cannot be achieved. In a word he is compelled to represent not his party nor his class, but the class for whom conditions are ripe for domination. In the interests of the movement itself, he is compelled to defend the interests of an alien class,

and to feed his own class with phrases and promises, with the assertion that the interests of that alien class are their own interests. Whoever puts himself in this awkward position is irrevocably lost.[29]

Only the expansion of the revolution could have spared Bolshevism from this tragic fate. And on this probability Bolshevism hinged its fate. Only abstentionists and cowards could advise the Bolsheviks not to go to the limit of the revolutionary potentialities of the Russian proletariat for fear of finding themselves at the end of the cul de sac. Revolutionary dynamism and international perspectives beat in the heart of Bolshevism.

The inherent danger of substitutionism

However, if the state built by the Bolshevik Party reflected not only the will of the party but of the total social reality in which the Bolsheviks in power found themselves, one should not draw the conclusion that there was no causal connection at all between Bolshevik centralism based on hierarchy of professional revolutionaries and the Stalinism of the future. Let us look at this question somewhat more closely.

The fact that a revolutionary party is at all needed for the socialist revolution shows that there is an unevenness in the level of culture and consciousness of different sections and groups of workers. If the working class were ideologically a homogeneous class there would not have been any need for leadership. Alas, the revolution would not wait until all the masses had reached a certain intellectual level, or level of class consciousness. Oppressed by capitalism, materially as well as spiritually, different sections of the workers show different levels of class independence. If not for this difference in consciousness among different sections of the working class, the capitalist class in the advanced countries would hardly find any social basis for itself. Under such conditions the class struggle would be the smoothest act of gradual progress. There would indeed scarcely be any class struggle to speak of; instead workers face the antagonism of other workers—the threat of strike breakers (workers) and policemen and soldiers (workers in uniform). If the working class were homogeneous there would not be the need for a workers' state either: after the revolution, the power of coercion would be unnecessary. Alas, the revolution has nothing in common with such anarchist-liberal daydreaming. Working-class discipline presumes, under capitalism and immediately after the proletarian revolution, not only the existence of more advanced and less advanced workers, ie the existence of leadership, but also the combination of conviction and coercion—the working class cannot free itself at a stroke from the birthmarks of capitalist barbarism.

Under capitalism, discipline confronts the worker as an external coercive power, as the power which capital has over him. Under socialism discipline will be the result of consciousness. It will become the habit of a free people. In the transition period it will be the outcome of the unity of the two elements—consciousness and coercion. Collective ownership of the means of production by the workers, ie the ownership by the workers' state of the means of production, will be the basis for the conscious element in labour discipline. At the same time the working class as a collective, through its institutions—soviets, trade unions, etc—will appear as a coercive power as regards the disciplining of the individual workers in production.

This conflict between the individual and the collective, the necessity of uniting conviction with its ugly opposite, coercion, the compulsion on the working class to use barbaric methods remaining from capitalism to fight capitalist barbarism, is but another affirmation that the workers are not liberated spiritually under capitalism, and would take a whole historical period to grow to full human stature. Agreeing with the anarchists that the state, even the workers' state, is an ugly offspring of class society and that real human history will start only by having a really consistent workers' state, it is nonetheless only on this basis that the state will ultimately wither away.

The fact that the working class needs a party or parties is in itself a proof of the cleavages in the working class. The more backward culturally, the weaker the organisation and self administration of the workers generally, the greater will be the intellectual cleavage between the class and its Marxist party. From this unevenness in the working class flows the great danger of an autonomous development of the party and its machine till it becomes, instead of the servant of the class, its master. This unevenness is a main source of the danger of 'substitutionism'.

The history of Bolshevism prior to the revolution is eloquent with Lenin's struggle against this danger. How often he appealed to the mass of the workers—especially in the stormy months of 1917—against the vacillating, compromising party leadership and its machine. As Trotsky so correctly summed up the interrelation between Lenin, the masses and the party machine:

Lenin was strong not only because he understood the laws of the class struggle but also because his ear was faultlessly attuned to the stirrings of the masses in motion. He represented not so much the party machine as the vanguard of the proletariat. He was definitely convinced that thousands from amongst those workers who had borne the brunt of supporting the underground party would now support him. The masses at the moment were more revolutionary than the party, and the party more revolutionary than its machine. As early as March the actual attitude of the workers and soldiers had in many cases become stormily apparent, and it was widely at variance with the instructions issued by all the parties, including the Bolshevik... On the other hand, the authority of the party machine, like its conservatism, was only in the making at that time. Lenin exerted influence not so much as an individual but because he embodied the influence of the class on the party and of the party on its machine.[30]

Men and women make history, and if they are organised in a party, they will have a greater impact on history than their relative number warrants. Nevertheless they alone do not make history and, for better or worse, they alone are not the cause of their greater specific weight, nor of the general history of the class, nor even of themselves in this class. In the final analysis, the only weapons to fight the 'substitutionism' of the revolutionary party for the class, and hence the transformation of the former into a conservative force, is the activity of the class itself, and its pressure not only against its social enemy, but also against its own agent, its party.

This is not the place to point out how far Trotsky in practice went in turning a necessity into a virtue, to what extremes of generalisation he turned to justify anti-democratic, anti-working-class, 'substitutionist' practices.

It is enough to mention his arguments in 1921 for the 'militarisation of labour'—compulsory labour imposed by the state. The trade unions, he said, should be statified. We need:

a new type of trade unionist, the energetic and imaginative economic organiser who will approach economic issues not from the angle of distribution and consumption but from that of expanding production, who will view them not with the eyes of somebody accustomed to confront the soviet government with demands and to bargain, but with the eyes of the true economic organiser.[31]

What about the defence of workers from the state, even from the workers' state? Can the trade unions neglect this? Trotsky did not answer the question, did not even pose it.

He said at the Ninth Congress that militarisation:

> is unthinkable without the militarisation of the trade unions as such, without the establishment of a regime in which every worker feels himself a soldier of labour, who cannot dispose of himself freely; if the order is given to transfer him, he must carry it out; if he does not carry it out, he will be a deserter who is punished. Who looks after this? The trade union. It creates the new regime. This is the militarisation of the working class.[32]

To cap his 'substitutionist' attitude Trotsky went as far as to say in 1924:

> None of us desires or is able to dispute the will of the party. The party in the last analysis is always right, because the party is the single historical instrument given to the proletariat for the solution of its basic problems. I have already said that in front of one's own party nothing could be easier than to acknowledge a mistake, nothing easier than to say: All my criticisms, my statements, my warnings, my protests—the whole thing was simply a mistake. I cannot say that, however, comrades, because I do not think it. I know that one must not be right *against* the party. One can be right only with the party, and through the party, for history has no other road for being in the right. The English have a saying: 'my country—right or wrong'. With far more historical justification we may say: my party—in certain concrete cases—right or wrong... And if the party adopts a decision which one or another of us thinks unjust, he will say: Just or unjust it is my party, and I shall support the consequences of the decision to the end.[33]

Substitutionism today

As a point of departure for an evaluation of the role of the revolutionary party in its relation to the working class, we cannot but return to the *Communist Manifesto*'s statement:

> All previous historical movements were movements of minorities or in the interests of minorities. The proletarian movement is the self conscious independent movement of the immense majority, in the interests of the immense majority.

From the much higher cultural level of the workers in the industrial countries than in Russia, their greater self reliance and organisational habits and the relatively greater social homogeneity of the mass of the toilers in these countries (not engulfed by hordes of peasants) one may deduce that prior to the revolution, during it and after its victory, the unevenness in consciousness of the masses will be much smaller than it was in Russia, although it will not have disappeared completely.

From this a number of conclusions may be drawn.

First, about the size of the revolutionary party as compared with that of the working class as a whole. In October 1906 the Russian Social Democratic Workers Party (including both Bolshevik and Menshevik factions) numbered 70,000. At the same time the Jewish Bund numbered 33,000, the Polish Social Democrats 28,000 and the Lettish Social Democrats 13,000. Altogether then, the *illegal* socialist parties numbered 144,000.[34] In August 1917 the Bolshevik Party had 200,000 members. On average, in 25 towns 5.4 percent of the industrial workers were members of the Bolshevik Party."[35] If the proportion of party members among the working class were the same in the advanced countries as it was in 1917, or 1905, in Russia, the party would have to have millions of members.

Because the unevenness in consciousness and culture is smaller in the advanced countries than it was in Russia, the relative size of the party should be even larger than it was in Russia. (The legality of the workers' parties also contributes to this.) Anyone who draws the opposite conclusion from the *actual* size of the reformist parties does not understand the real role of the masses in the revolutionary struggle. The reformist party is in the main an apparatus for attracting votes in parliamentary and other elections. Hence it does not need a really active mass membership. On the whole the supporters of such a party do not find it necessary to join it actively, or to read its press. Active support of the masses for a revolutionary party must lead to a comparatively much greater number of workers joining it.

From this it is clear that little groups cannot in any way substitute for the mass revolutionary party, let alone for the mass of the working class.[36]

Now what about the relation between the revolutionary party and the class?

Every party, whether reformist or revolutionary, whether conservative or liberal, aims to get support in order to lead towards one aim or another. The revolutionary workers' party also aims to lead. But here the similarity stops. The methods by which this leadership is established and the nature of the leadership are totally different.

One can visualise three kinds of leadership that, for lack of better names we shall call: those of the teacher, the foreman and the companion in struggle. The first kind of leadership shown by small sects is 'blackboard socialism' (in Britain an extreme example of this sort is the Socialist Party of Great Britain, in which didactic methods take the place of participation in struggle). The second kind, with foreman-worker or officer-soldier relations, characterises all bureaucratic reformist and Stalinist parties: the leadership sits in a caucus and decides what they will tell the workers to do, without the workers actively participating. What characterises both these kinds of leadership is the fact that directives go only one way: the leaders conduct a monologue with the masses.

The third kind of leadership is analogous to that between a strike committee and the workers on strike, or a shop steward and their mates. The revolutionary party must conduct a dialogue with the workers outside it.[37] The party, in consequence, should not invent tactics out of thin air, but put as its first duty to *learn* from the experience of the mass movement and then generalise from it. The great events of working-class history have shown the correctness of this emphasis beyond all measure of doubt. The workers of Paris in 1871 established a new form of state—a state without a standing army and bureaucracy, where all officials received the average worker's salary, with the right of recall of all officials, etc, *before* Marx began to generalise about the nature and structure of a workers' state. Again, the workers of Petrograd, in 1905, established a soviet independently of the Bolshevik Party, actually in opposition to the local Bolshevik leadership and in face of at least suspicion, if not animosity, on the part of Lenin himself. Therefore one cannot but agree with Rosa Luxemburg when she wrote in 1904:

> The main characteristics of the tactics of struggle of social democracy are not 'invented', but are the result of a continuous series of great creative acts of elementary class struggle. Here also the unconscious precedes the conscious, the logic of the objective historical process comes before the subjective logic of its bearer.[38]

The role of the Marxists is to generalise the living, evolving experience of the class struggle, to give a conscious expression to the instinctive drive of the working class to reorganise society on a socialist basis.

Because the working class is far from being monolithic, and because the path to socialism is uncharted, wide differences of strategy and tactics can and should exist in the revolutionary party. The alternative is the bureaucratised party or the sect with its 'leader'. Here one cannot but regret Trotsky's sweeping statement that 'any serious factional fight in a party is always in the final analysis a reflection of the class struggle'.[39] This verges on a vulgar materialist interpretation of human thought as growing directly out of material conditions! What class pressures separated Lenin from Luxemburg, or Trotsky from Lenin (1903-1917), or what changes in class pressures can one see in Plekhanov's zigzags: with Lenin in 1903, against him in 1903, against him in 1905, then with him again and at last breaking, it is true, with Lenin and with the revolutionary movement and joining the class enemy? Can the differences in the theory of imperialism between Lenin and Luxemburg be derived from an analysis of their position in class society? Scientific socialism must live and thrive on controversy. And scientists who start off with the same basic assumptions, and then use the same method of analysis, do differ in all fields of research.

In order that the party should be able to conduct a dialogue with the masses, it is necessary not only that the party have confidence in the tremendous abilities of the working class in action, but also that the party understands correctly the situation in the country and the conditions of the working class, materially and morally. Any self deceit on its part must cut short the dialogue and turn it into a boring monologue.

The party has to be subordinated to the whole. And so the internal regime in the revolutionary party must be subordinated to the relation between the party and the class. The managers of factories can discuss their business in secret and then put before the workers a fait accompli. The revolutionary party that seeks to overthrow capitalism cannot accept the notion of a discussion on policies inside the party without the participation of the mass of the workers—policies which are then brought 'unanimously' ready made to the class. Since the revolutionary party cannot have interests apart from the class, all the party's issues of policy are those of the class, and they should therefore be thrashed out in the open, in its presence. The freedom of discussion which exists in the factory meeting, which aims at unity of action after decisions are taken, should apply to the revolutionary party. This means that all discussions on basic issues of policy should be discussed in the light of day, in the open press. Let the mass of the workers take part in the discussion, put pressure on the party, its apparatus and leadership.[40]

Above all, the revolutionary party should follow the guide of the *Communist Manifesto* when it says:

> In what relation do the communists stand to the proletarians as a whole? The communists do not form a separate party opposed to other working-class parties. They have no interests separate and apart from the proletariat as a whole. They do not set up any sectarian principles of their own, by which to shape and mould the proletarian movement. The communists are distinguished from other working class parties by this only: (1) In the national struggles of the proletarians of the different countries, they point out and bring to the front the common interests of the entire proletariat, independently of all nationality. (2) In the various stages of development which the struggle of the working-class against the bourgeoisie has to pass through, they always and everywhere represent the interests of the movement as a whole. The communists, therefore, are on the one hand, practically, the most advanced and resolute section of the working-class parties of every country, that section which pushes forward all others: on the other hand, theoretically, they have over the great mass of the proletariat the advantage of clearly understanding the line of march, the conditions, and the ultimate general results of the proletarian movement.

The *whole* of the working class will have to mix its level of consciousness and organisation, through a prolonged struggle, including a struggle of ideas. As Marx said to revolutionaries who flattered the German workers in his time:

> While we say to the workers: you have 15 or 20 years of bourgeois and national wars to go through, not merely to alter conditions but to alter yourselves and make yourselves fit to take political power, you tell them on the contrary that they must take over political power at once or abandon all hope.

1   N Trotsky, *Nashi Politicheskye Zadachi* (Geneva, 1904) p54.

2   Ibid, p105, quoted in I Deutscher, *The Prophet Armed* (London, 1954) pp92-93.

3   V I Lenin, *Sochinenya*, IX, p14.

4   L Kritsman, *Geroicheskii Period Velikoi Russkoi Revolutsii* (Moscow, 1924) pp133-136.

5   *Chetvertyi Vserossiikii Sezd Professionalnykh Soyuzov*, Vol 1, 1921, pp66, 119.

6   *Vtoroi Vserossiikii Sezd Professionalnykh Soyuzov*, 1921, p 138.

7   V I Lenin, *Sochinenya*, XXVI, p394.

8   VKP (b) *v Rezoliutsiakh*, 4th ed, Vol 1, p126.

9   Ibid, 6th ed, Vol 1, pp154-60.

10   L Trotsky, *History of the Russian Revolution* (London, 1932) Vol 1, p59.

11   Ibid, and Lenin, *Sochinenya*, XXI, p432.

12   A Shliapnikov, *The Year Seventeen*, in Russian, (Moscow, 1924) Vol 1, p197.

13   A S Bubnov and others, VPK (b) (Moscow-Leningrad, 1931) p113.

14   *Pravda*, 15 March 1917, quoted in Trotsky, op cit, p305.

15   *Pravda*, 8 April 1917.

16   A S Bubnov, op cit, p114.

17   VKP (b) *v Rezoliutsiakh*, 4th ed, Vol 1, p258.

18   V I Lenin, *Sochinenya*, 3rd ed, XX, p652.

19   Ibid, XXI, p526.

20   L Trotsky, *Stalin* (London, 1947), pp341-342.

21   A S Bubnov, op cit, p511.

22   Ibid p512.

23   *9 Sezd*, RKP(b), p52.

24   Ibid, pp62-63.

25   Ibid, pp56-57.

26   *11 Sezd*, RKP (b), p83.

27   Ibid, p134.

28   *12 Sezd*, RKP (b), p133.

29   F Engels, *The Peasant War in Germany* (London, 1927) pp135-136.

30   L Trotsky, *Stalin* (London, 1947) p201. It is sad to point out that when Trotsky dealt with the question of the dangers of bureaucratic conservatism in the Trotskyist organisations he pooh-poohed the idea, taking flight in a simplistic materialist interpretation of bureaucratism. When J P Cannon, the American Trotskyist leader, was accused of bureaucratic conservatism, Trotsky said that the accusation was 'a bare psychological abstraction insofar as no specific social interests are shown underlying this "conservatism".' (L Trotsky, *In Defense of Marxism* (New York, 1942) p81.) What special social interests were underlying the 'committee-men' of pre-1917, of which Stalin was the archetype? Trotsky didn't try to show this—quite rightly—in his last work, *Stalin*, whose central theme is the conservative, anti-democratic nature of the 'committee-men'.

31   Trotsky quoted in Deutscher, *Soviet Trade Unions* (London, 1950), p42.

32   *9 Sezd*, RKP (b), p101.

33   *13 Sezd*, RKP (b), pp 165-166. Trotsky's and Lenin's attitude to the Kronstadt rebellion is often quoted by Mensheviks, anarchists and also some other left critics of Trotsky and Lenin as an example of bureaucratic oppression. Actually the main aspect of Kronstadt was a peasant and semipeasant rebellion against the towns. Hence all the inner party oppositions—including the Workers' Opposition of Shliapnikov and Kollontai—took an active part in its suppression, and in its footsteps came the policy of concessions to petty capitalism, to the peasantry—the New Economic Policy (NEP). However the question of Kronstadt as well as the different opposition groups which existed prior to Trotsky's going into opposition, and which in 1923 joined him under his leadership, is a fascinating study which deserves a separate study.

34   V I Lenin, *Sochinenya*, X, p483.

35   *6 Sezd*, RKP (b), (Moscow, 1958) p390.

36   Nobody in Russia doubted that Trotsky's group alone—the Mezhrayonka—which in August 1917 had some 4,000 members was much too small to be able seriously to affect the march of events. Similarly one can understand Trotsky when in 1921 he referred to the Communist Workers' Party of Germany (KAPD) as being slight: 'no more than 30,000-40,000' members (L Trotsky, *The First Five Years of the Communist International* (London, 1953) Vol 2, p26).

37   As Rosa Luxemburg put it: 'Of course through the theoretical analysis of the social conditions of struggle, social democracy has introduced the element of consciousness into the proletarian class struggle to an unprecedented degree; it gave the class struggle its clarity of aim; it created, for the first time, a permanent mass workers' organisation, and thus built a firm backbone for the class struggle. However it would be catastrophically wrong for us to assume that from now on all the historical initiative of the people has passed to the hands of the social democratic organisation alone, and that the unorganised mass of the proletariat has turned into a formless thing, into the deadweight of history. On the contrary, the popular masses continue to be the living matter of world history, even in the presence of social democracy, and only if there is blood circulation between the organised nucleus and the popular masses, only if one heartbeat vitalises the two, can social democracy prove that it is capable of great historical deeds' *Leipziger Volkszeitung*, June 1913, pp 26-28.

38   *Die Neue Zeit*, 1904, p491.

39   L Trotsky, *In Defence of Marxism* (New York, 1942), p60.

40   Some cases of secrecy are justified and every worker will understand this. Just as factory meetings can be closed to the capitalists and their media and other agents, so there are moments in the life of a revolutionary party which have to be kept secret. But in all cases the party should be able to justify this to the workers and convince them that no basic decisions of policy are being hidden from them.

The class, the party and the leadership

Leon Trotsky

The extent to which the working-class movement has been thrown backward may be gauged not only by the condition of the mass organisations but by ideological groupings and those theoretical inquiries in which so many groups are engaged. In Paris there is published a periodical *Que Faire* (What to do) which for some reason considers itself Marxist but in reality remains completely within the framework of the empiricism of the left bourgeois intellectuals and those isolated workers who have assimilated all the vices of the intellectuals.

Like all groups lacking a scientific foundation, without a programme and without any tradition, this little periodical tried to hang on to the coat tails of the POUM—which seemed to open the shortest avenue to the masses and to victory. But the result of these ties with the Spanish revolution seems at first entirely unexpected: the periodical did not advance but on the contrary retrogressed. As a matter of fact, this is wholly in the nature of things. The contradictions between the petty bourgeoisie's conservatism and the needs of the proletarian revolution have developed in the extreme. It is only natural that the defenders and interpreters of the policies of the POUM found themselves thrown far back both in political and theoretical fields.

The periodical *Que Faire* is in and of itself of no importance whatever. But it is of symptomatic interest. That is why we think it profitable to dwell upon this periodical's appraisal of the causes for the collapse of the Spanish revolution, inasmuch as this appraisal discloses very graphically the fundamental features now prevailing in the left flank of pseudo-Marxism.

We begin with a verbatim quotation from a review of the pamphlet *Spain Betrayed*, by comrade Casanova: 'Why was the revolution crushed? Because', replies the author (Casanova), 'the Communist Party conducted a false policy which was unfortunately followed by the revolutionary masses.' But why, in the devil's name, did the revolutionary masses who left their former leaders rally to the banner of the Communist Party? 'Because there was no genuinely revolutionary party.' We are presented with a pure tautology. A false policy of the masses; an immature party either manifests a certain condition of social forces (immaturity of the working class, lack of independence of the peasantry) which must be explained by proceeding from facts, presented among others by Casanova himself; or it is the product of the actions of certain malicious individuals or groups of individuals, actions which do not correspond to the efforts of 'sincere individuals' alone capable of saving the revolution. After groping for the first and Marxist road, Casanova takes the second. We are ushered into the domain of pure demonology; the criminal responsible for the defeat is the chief devil, Stalin, abetted by the anarchists and all the other little devils; the god of revolutionists unfortunately did not send a Lenin or a Trotsky to Spain as he did in Russia in 1917.

The conclusion then follows: 'This is what comes of seeking at any cost to force the ossified orthodoxy of a chapel upon facts.' This theoretical haughtiness is made all the more significant by the fact that it is hard to imagine how so great a number of banalities, vulgarisms and mistakes quite specifically of a conservative philistine type could be compressed into so few lines.

The author of the above quotation avoids giving any explanation for the defeat of the Spanish revolution; he only indicates that profound explanations, like the 'condition of social forces', are necessary. The evasion of any explanation is not accidental. These critics of Bolshevism are all theoretical cowards, for the simple reason that they have nothing solid under their feet. In order not to reveal their own bankruptcy they juggle facts and prowl around the opinions of others. They confine themselves to hints and halfthoughts as if they just haven't the time to delineate their full wisdom. As a matter of fact they possess no wisdom at all. Their haughtiness is lined with intellectual charlatanism.

Let us analyse step by step the hints and half thoughts of our author. According to him a false policy of the masses can be explained only as it 'manifests a certain condition of social forces', namely, the immaturity of the working class and the lack of independence of the peasantry. Anyone searching for tautologies couldn't find in general a flatter one. A 'false policy of the masses' is explained by the 'immaturity' of the masses. But what is 'immaturity' of the masses? Obviously, their predisposition to false policies. Of just what the false policy consisted, and who were its initiators; the masses or the leaders—that is passed over in silence by our author. By means of a tautology he unloads the responsibility on the masses. This classical trick of all traitors, deserters and their attorneys is especially revolting in connection with the Spanish proletariat.

In July 1936—not to refer to an earlier period—the Spanish workers repelled the assault of the officers who had prepared their conspiracy under the protection of the People's Front. The masses improvised militias and created workers' committees, the strongholds of their future dictatorship. The leading organisations of the proletariat on the other hand helped the bourgeoisie to destroy these committees, to liquidate the assaults of the workers on private property and to subordinate the workers' militias to the command of the bourgeoisie, with the POUM moreover participating in the government and assuming direct responsibility for this work of the counter-revolution. What does 'immaturity' of the proletariat signify in this case? Self evidently only this, that despite the correct political line chosen by the masses, the latter were unable to smash the coalition of socialists, Stalinists, anarchists and the POUM with the bourgeoisie. This piece of sophistry takes as its starting point a concept of some absolute maturity, ie a perfect condition of the masses in which they do not require a correct leadership, and, more than that, are capable of conquering against their own leadership. There is not and there cannot be such maturity.

Our sages object: but why should workers who show such correct revolutionary instinct and such superior fighting qualities submit to treacherous leadership? Our answer is: There wasn't even a hint of mere subordination. The workers' line of march at all times cut a certain angle to the line of the leadership. And at the most critical moments this angle became 180 degrees. The leadership then helped directly or indirectly to subdue the workers by armed force.

In May 1937 the workers of Catalonia rose not only without their own leadership but against it. The anarchist leaders—pathetic and contemptible bourgeois masquerading cheaply as revolutionists—have repeated hundreds of times in their press that, had the CNT wanted to take power and set up their dictatorship in May, they could have done so without any difficulty. This time the anarchist leaders speak the unadulterated truth. The POUM leadership actually dragged at the tail of the CNT, only they covered up their policy with a different phraseology. It was thanks to this and this alone that the bourgeoisie succeeded in crushing the May uprising of the 'immature' proletariat. One must understand exactly nothing in the sphere of the interrelationships between the class and the party, between the masses and the leaders in order to repeat the hollow statement that the Spanish masses merely followed their leaders. The only thing that can be said is that the masses who sought at all times to blast their way to the correct road found no new leadership corresponding to the demands of the revolution. Before us is a profoundly dynamic process, with the various stages of the revolution shifting swiftly, with the leadership or various sections of the leadership quickly deserting to the side of the class enemy, and our sages engage in a purely static discussion: why did the working class as a whole follow a bad leadership?

There is an ancient, evolutionary-liberal epigram: every people gets the government it deserves. History, however, shows that one and the same people may in the course of a comparatively brief epoch get very different governments (Russia, Italy, Germany, Spain, etc) and furthermore that the order of these governments doesn't at all proceed in one and the same direction: from despotism—to freedom, as was imagined by the evolutionist liberals. The secret is this, that a people is comprised of hostile classes, and the classes themselves are comprised of different and in part antagonistic layers which fall under different leadership; furthermore every people falls under the influence of other peoples who are likewise comprised of classes. Governments do not express the systematically growing 'maturity' of a 'people' but are the product of the struggle between different classes and the different layers within one and the same class, and, finally, the action of external forces—alliances, wars and so on. To this should be added that a government once it has established itself, may endure much longer than the relationship of forces which produced it. It is precisely out of this historical contradiction that revolutions, coup d'états, counter-revolutions, etc arise.

The very same dialectical approach is necessary in dealing with the question of the leadership of a class. Imitating the liberals our sages tacitly accept the axiom that every class gets the leadership it deserves. In reality leadership is not at all a mere 'reflection' of a class or the product of its own free creativeness. A leadership is shaped in the process of clashes between the different classes or the friction between the different layers within a given class. Having once arisen, the leadership invariably rises above its class and thereby becomes predisposed to the pressure and influence of other classes. The proletariat may 'tolerate' for a long time a leadership that has already suffered a complete inner degeneration but has not as yet had the opportunity to express this degeneration amid great events. A great historic shock is necessary to reveal sharply the contradiction between the leadership and the class.

The mightiest historical shocks are wars and revolutions. Precisely for this reason the working class is often caught unawares by war and revolution. But even in cases where the old leadership has revealed its internal corruption, the class cannot improvise immediately a new leadership, especially if it has not inherited from the previous period strong revolutionary cadres capable of utilising the collapse of the old leading party. The Marxist, ie dialectical and not scholastic interpretation of the inter-relationship between a class and its leadership does not leave a single stone unturned of our author's legalistic sophistry.

He conceives of the proletariat's maturity as something purely static. Yet during a revolution the consciousness of a class is the most dynamic process directly determining the course of the revolution. Was it possible in January 1917 or even in March, after the overthrow of tsarism, to give an answer to the question whether the Russian proletariat had sufficiently 'matured' for the conquest of power in eight to nine months? The working class was at that time extremely heterogeneous socially and politically. During the years of the war it had been renewed by 30-40 percent from the ranks of the petty bourgeoisie, often reactionary, at the expense of backward peasants, at the expense of women and youth. The Bolshevik Party in March 1917 was followed by an insignificant minority of the working class and furthermore there was discord within the party itself. The overwhelming majority of the workers supported the Mensheviks and the 'Social Revolutionaries', ie conservative social patriots. The situation was even less favourable with regard to the army and the peasantry. We must add to this: the general low level of culture in the country, the lack of political experience among the broadest layers of the proletariat, especially in the provinces, let alone the peasants and soldiers.

What was the 'active' [untranslatable term, which means in part 'liquid assets'—translator] of Bolshevism? A clear and thoroughly thought out revolutionary conception at the beginning of the revolution was held only by Lenin. The Russian cadres of the party were scattered and to a considerable degree bewildered. But the party had authority among the advanced workers. Lenin had great authority with the party cadres. Lenin's political conception corresponded to the actual development of the revolution and was reinforced by each new event. These elements of the 'active' worked wonders in a revolutionary situation, that is, in conditions of bitter class struggle. The party quickly aligned its policy to correspond with Lenin's conception, to correspond that is with the actual course of the revolution. Thanks to this it met with firm support among tens of thousands of advanced workers. Within a few months, by basing itself upon the development of the revolution the party was able to convince the majority of the workers of the correctness of its slogans. This majority, organised into Soviets, was able in its turn to attract the soldiers and peasants.

How can this dynamic, dialectical process be exhausted by a formula of the maturity or immaturity of the proletariat? A colossal factor in the maturity of the Russian proletariat in February or March 1917 was Lenin. He did not fall from the skies. He personified the revolutionary tradition of the working class. For Lenin's slogans to find their way to the masses there had to exist cadres, even though numerically small at the beginning; there had to exist the confidence of the cadres in the leadership, a confidence based on the entire experience of the past. To cancel these elements from one's calculations is simply to ignore the living revolution, to substitute for it an abstraction, the 'relationship of forces', because the development of the revolution precisely consists of this, that the relationship of forces keeps incessantly and rapidly changing under the impact of the changes in the consciousness of the proletariat, the attraction of backward layers to the advanced, the growing assurance of the class in its own strength. The vital mainspring in this process is the party, just as the vital mainspring in the mechanism of the party is its leadership. The role and the responsibility of the leadership in a revolutionary epoch are colossal.

The October victory is a serious testimonial to the 'maturity' of the proletariat. But this maturity is relative. A few years later the very same proletariat permitted the revolution to be strangled by a bureaucracy which rose from its ranks. Victory is not at all the ripe fruit of the proletariat's 'maturity'. Victory is a strategical task. It is necessary to utilise in order to mobilise the masses; taking as a starting point the given level of their 'maturity' it is necessary to propel them forward, teach them to understand that the enemy is by no means omnipotent, that it is torn asunder with contradictions, that behind the imposing facade panic prevails. Had the Bolshevik Party failed to carry out this work, there couldn't even be talk of the victory of the proletarian revolution. The soviets would have been crushed by the counter-revolution, and the little sages of all countries would have written articles and books on the keynote that only uprooted visionaries could dream in Russia of the dictatorship of the proletariat, so small numerically and so immature.

Equally abstract, pedantic and false is the reference to the 'lack of independence' of the peasantry. When and where did our sage ever observe in capitalist society a peasantry with an independent revolutionary programme or a capacity for independent revolutionary initiative? The peasantry can play a very great role in the revolution, but only an auxiliary role.

In many instances the Spanish peasants acted boldly and fought courageously. But to rouse the entire mass of the peasantry, the proletariat had to set an example of a decisive uprising against the bourgeoisie and inspire the peasants with faith in the possibility of victory. In the meantime the revolutionary initiative of the proletariat itself was paralysed at every step by its own organisations.

The 'immaturity' of the proletariat, the 'lack of independence' of the peasantry are neither final nor basic factors in historical events. Underlying the consciousness of the classes are the classes themselves, their numerical strength, their role in economic life. Underlying the classes is a specific system of production which is determined in its turn by the level of the development of productive forces. Why not then say that the defeat of the Spanish proletariat was determined by the low level of technology?

Our author substitutes mechanistic determinism for the dialectic conditioning of the historical process. Hence the cheap jibes about the role of individuals, good and bad. History is a process of the class struggle. But classes do not bring their full weight to bear automatically and simultaneously. In the process of struggle the classes create various organs which play an important and independent role and are subject to deformations. This also provides the basis for the role of personalities in history. There are naturally great objective causes which created the autocratic rule of Hitler but only dull witted pedants of 'determinism' could deny today the enormous historic role of Hitler. The arrival of Lenin in Petrograd on 3 April 1917 turned the Bolshevik Party in time and enabled the party to lead the revolution to victory.

Our sages might say that, had Lenin died abroad at the beginning of 1917, the October Revolution would have taken place 'just the same'. But that is not so. Lenin represented one of the living elements of the historical process. He personified the experience and the perspicacity of the most active section of the proletariat. His timely appearance on the arena of the revolution was necessary in order to mobilise the vanguard and provide it with an opportunity to rally the working class and the peasant masses. Political leadership in the crucial moments of historical turns can become just as decisive a factor as is the role of the chief command during the critical moments of war. History is not an automatic process. Otherwise why leaders? Why parties? Why programmes? Why theoretical struggles?

'But why, in the devil's name,' asks the author, as we have already heard, 'did the revolutionary masses who left their former leaders, rally to the banner of the Communist Party?' The question is falsely posed. It is not true that the revolutionary masses left all of their former leaders. The workers who were previously connected with specific organisations continued to cling to them, while they observed and checked. Workers in general do not easily break with the party that awakens them to conscious life. Moreover the existence of mutual protection within the People's Front lulled them: since everybody agreed, everything must be all right. The new and fresh masses naturally turned to the Comintern as the party which had accomplished the only victorious proletarian revolution and which, it was hoped, was capable of assuring arms to Spain. Furthermore the Comintern was the most zealous champion of the idea of the People's Front; this inspired confidence among the inexperienced layers of workers. Within the People's Front the Comintern was the most zealous champion of the bourgeois character of the revolution; this inspired the confidence of the petty and in part the middle bourgeoisie. That is why the masses 'rallied to the banner of the Communist Party'.

Our author depicts the matter as if the proletariat were in a well stocked shoe store, selecting a new pair of boots. Even this simple operation, as is well known, does not always prove successful. As regards new leadership, the choice is very limited. Only gradually, only on the basis of their own experience through several stages can the broad layers of the masses become convinced that a new leadership is firmer, more reliable, more loyal than the old. To be sure, during a revolution, ie when events move swiftly, a weak party can quickly grow into a mighty one provided it lucidly understands the course of the revolution and possesses staunch cadres that do not become intoxicated with phrases and are not terrorised by persecution. But such a party must be available prior to the revolution inasmuch as the process of educating the cadres requires a considerable period of time and the revolution does not afford this time.

To the left of all the other parties in Spain stood the POUM, which undoubtedly embraced revolutionary proletarian elements not previously firmly tied to anarchism. But it was precisely this party that played a fatal role in the development of the Spanish revolution. It could not become a mass party because in order to do so it was first necessary to overthrow the old parties and it was possible to overthrow them only by an irreconcilable struggle, by a merciless exposure of their bourgeois character. Yet the POUM while criticising the old parties subordinated itself to them on all fundamental questions. It participated in the 'People's' election bloc; entered the government which liquidated workers' committees; engaged in a struggle to reconstitute this governmental coalition; capitulated time and again to the anarchist leadership; conducted, in connection with this, a false trade union policy; took a vacillating and non-revolutionary attitude towards the May 1937 uprising. From the standpoint of determinism in general it is possible of course to recognise that the policy of the POUM was not accidental. Everything in this world has its cause. However, the series of causes engendering the centrism of the POUM are by no means a mere reflection of the condition of the Spanish or Catalonian proletariat. Two causalities moved towards each other at an angle and at a certain moment they came into hostile conflict.

It is possible by taking into account previous international experi-ence, Moscow's influence, the influence of a number of defeats, etc, to explain politically and psychologically why the POUM unfolded as a centrist party. But this does not alter its centrist character, nor does it alter the fact that a centrist party invariably acts as a brake upon the revolution, must each time smash its own head, and may bring about the collapse of the revolution. It does not alter the fact that the Catalonian masses were far more revolutionary than the POUM, which in turn was more revolutionary than its leadership. In these conditions to unload the responsibility for false policies on the 'immaturity' of the masses is to engage in the sheer charlatanism frequently resorted to by political bankrupts.

The historical falsification consists in this, that the responsibility for the defeat of the Spanish masses is unloaded on the working masses and not those parties which paralysed or simply crushed the revolution-ary movement of the masses. The attorneys of the POUM simply deny the responsibility of the leaders, in order thus to escape shouldering their own responsibility. This impotent philosophy, which seeks to rec-oncile defeats as a necessary link in the chain of cosmic developments, is completely incapable of posing and refuses to pose the question of such concrete factors as programmes, parties, personalities that were the organisers of defeat. This philosophy of fatalism and prostration is diametrically opposed to Marxism as the theory of revolutionary action.

Civil war is a process wherein political tasks are solved by military means. Were the outcome of this war determined by the 'condition of class forces', the war itself would not be necessary. War has its own organisation, its own policies, its own methods, its own leadership by which its fate is directly determined. Naturally, the 'condition of class forces' supplies the foundation for all other political factors; but just as the foundation of a building does not reduce the importance of walls, windows, doors, roofs, so the 'condition of classes' does not invalidate the importance of parties, their strategy, their leadership. By dissolving the concrete in the abstract, our sages really halted midway. The most 'pro-found' solution of the problem would have been to declare the defeat of the Spanish proletariat as due to the inadequate development of produc-tive forces. Such a key is accessible to any fool.

By reducing to zero the significance of the party and of the leader-ship these sages deny in general the possibility of revolutionary victory.

Because there are not the least grounds for expecting conditions more favourable. Capitalism has ceased to advance, the proletariat does not grow numerically, on the contrary it is the army of unemployed that grows, which does not increase but reduces the fighting force of the proletariat and has a negative effect also upon its consciousness. There are similarly no grounds for believing that under the regime of capitalism the peasantry is capable of attaining a higher revolutionary consciousness. The conclusion from the analysis of our author is thus complete pessimism, a sliding away from revolutionary perspectives. It must be said—to do them justice—that they do not themselves understand what they say.

As a matter of fact, the demands they make upon the consciousness of the masses are utterly fantastic. The Spanish workers, as well as the Spanish peasants, gave the maximum of what these classes are able to give in a revolutionary situation. We have in mind precisely the class of millions and tens of millions.

Que Faire represents merely one of these little schools, or churches or chapels who, frightened by the course of the struggle and the onset of reaction, publish their little journals and their theoretical études in a corner, on the sidelines away from the actual developments of revolutionary thought, let alone the movement of the masses.

The Spanish proletariat fell the victim of a coalition composed of imperialists, Spanish republicans, socialists, anarchists, Stalinists and, on the left flank, the POUM. They all paralysed the socialist revolution which the Spanish proletariat had actually begun to realise. It is not easy to dispose of the socialist revolution. No one has yet devised other methods than ruthless repressions, massacre of the vanguard, execution of the leaders, etc. The POUM of course did not want this. It wanted on the one hand to participate in the Republican government and to enter as a loyal peace loving opposition into the general bloc of ruling parties; and on the other hand to achieve peaceful comradely relations at a time when it was a question of implacable civil war. For this very reason the POUM fell victim to the contradictions of its own policy. The most consistent policy in the ruling bloc was pursued by the Stalinists. They were the fighting vanguard of the bourgeois-republican counter-revolution. They wanted to eliminate the need of fascism by proving to the Spanish and world bourgeoisie that they were themselves capable of strangling the proletarian revolution under the banner of 'democracy'. This was the gist of their policies. The bankrupts of the Spanish People's Front are today trying to unload the blame on the GPU. I trust that we cannot be suspected of leniency towards the crimes of the GPU. But we see clearly and we tell the workers that the GPU acted in this instance only as the most resolute detachment in the service of the People's Front. Therein was the strength of the GPU, therein was the historic role of Stalin. Only ignorant philistines can wave this aside with stupid little jokes about the chief devil.

These gentlemen do not even bother with the question of the social character of the revolution. Moscow's lackeys, for the benefit of England and France, proclaimed the Spanish revolution as bourgeois. Upon this fraud were erected the perfidious policies of the People's Front, policies which would have been completely false even if the Spanish revolution had really been bourgeois. But from the very beginning the revolution expressed much more graphically its proletarian character than did the revolution of 1917 in Russia. In the leadership of the POUM gentlemen sit today who consider that the policy of Andreas Nin was too 'leftist', that the really correct thing was to have remained the left flank of the People's Front. Victor Serge, who is in a hurry to compromise himself by a frivolous attitude towards serious questions, writes that Nin did not wish to submit to commands from Oslo or Coyoacan. Can a serious man really be capable of reducing to petty gossip the problem of the class content of a revolution?

The sages of *Que Faire* have no answer whatever to this question. They do not understand the question itself. Of what significance indeed is the fact that the 'immature' proletariat founded its own organs of power, seized enterprises, sought to regulate production, while the POUM tried with all its might to keep from breaking with bourgeois anarchists who, in an alliance with the bourgeois republicans and the no less bourgeois socialists and Stalinists, assaulted and strangled the proletarian revolution? Such 'trifles' are obviously of interest only to representatives of 'ossified orthodoxy'. The sages of *Que Faire* possess instead a special apparatus which measures the maturity of the proletariat and the relationship of forces independently of all questions of revolutionary class strategy.

What is sectarianism?

Duncan Hallas

The term sectarianism is used so loosely that it may be as well to start by clarifying what it does not mean. It is sometimes asserted that it is sectarian to try to build your own organization in the course of intervention in various struggles. This is nonsense. If you believe that your organization's politics are correct, or at least more correct than those of others, you will naturally want it to grow and will try to build it. Otherwise you are not politically serious.

Of course, this may sometimes be attempted in an arrogant or insensitive fashion (not, I hope, by SWP members, or not very often), but that is not so much sectarianism as stupidity.

Sectarianism refers *exclusively* to erroneous attitudes to the class struggle.

"By directing socialism towards a fusion with the working-class movement," wrote Lenin, "Karl Marx and Frederick Engels did their greatest service: They created a revolutionary theory that explained the necessity for this fusion and gave socialists the task of organizing the class struggle of the proletariat."

Fusion, in this context, does not mean the dissolution of a revolutionary organization into a non-revolutionary one. Lenin was totally committed to building a revolutionary organization and broke ruthlessly with those, including many of his former collaborators, who wavered on this central point. The key words are "the class struggle of the proletariat." It is with this that socialists must "fuse."

The notion goes back to *The Communist Manifesto*. Sectarians, for Marx and Engels, were those who created "utopias," abstract schemes derived from supposed general principles, to which people were to be won by persuasion and example—cooperative "islands of socialism" and suchlike—as opposed to the Marxist emphasis on "the real movement," the actual class struggle. It was with this in mind that Marx wrote: "The sect sees the justification for its existence and its point of honor not in what it has in common with the class movement but in the particular shibboleth which distinguishes it from the movement." (The emphasis is Marx's own.)

Class movement is meant literally. It is not a matter, or not primarily a matter, of this or that working-class institution but of the course of development of the real class struggle and the development of class consciousness. Marx was a revolutionary. For him revolution was not a "particular shibboleth," but a necessary stage in the struggle for socialism which, in turn, can only be based on the class struggle, regardless, as he wrote, of "what this or that proletarian, or even the whole of the proletariat at the moment considers as its aim."

However, sectarianism is not necessarily avoided by formal acceptance of the centrality of the class struggle. As early as the 1880s Engels was ridiculing the German Marxist émigrés in the USA for turning Marxism into "a kind of 'only-salvation' dogma and [keeping] aloof from any movement which did not accept that dogma." Engels had in mind the Knights of Labor, a considerable, although confused, attempt at working-class organization, which, he argued (vainly, as far as the German American Marxists were concerned) "ought not to be poohpoohed from without but revolutionized from within."

The argument applies generally. So, in the early years of the Communist International, a good number of genuine revolutionaries, mainly in Germany but not only there, were opposed to systematic work in the existing unions. Their argument was that these unions were bureaucratized and conservative, if not downright reactionary. It was broadly true. It was also true that these unions organized millions of workers and, however bureaucratized and reactionary their leadership, they were class organizations that necessarily played a role (a bad one) in the class struggle and could not simply be bypassed. As Lenin wrote:

> We are waging the struggle against the opportunist and social-chauvinist leaders in order to win the working class over to our side. It would be absurd to forget this most elementary and most self-evident truth. Yet this is the very absurdity that the German "Left" Communists perpetrate when, *because* of the reactionary and counter-revolutionary character of

the trade unions' top leadership, they jump to the conclusion that—we must withdraw from the trade unions, refuse to work in them, and create new and *artificial* forms of labor organization! This is so unpardonable a blunder that it is tantamount to the greatest service Communists could render the bourgeoisie.

The common thread between this mistake by the (for the most part) active and revolutionary "lefts" and all other forms of sectarianism is failure to relate to the *concrete* struggles of workers, however difficult it may be to do so, and to set up utopian schemes as alternatives.

Thus, the propagandistic forms of sectarianism, very different at first sight, have this same root. There is a rich (if that is the appropriate word) experience of this in Britain. We may call them "the pure selected few" sectarians after a verse by the late Tommy Jackson, referring to the British Socialist Labour Party (SLP):

> We are the pure selected few
> And all the rest are damned
> There's room enough in hell for you
> We don't want heaven crammed.

The SLP, although by no means the worst of its kind, placed excessive emphasis on propaganda and a very high level of formal (Marxist) training as a condition of membership. Not so surprisingly, it also believed in separate "red unions" and had a rule forbidding members to hold union office, although they were allowed to be cardholders where "job necessity" (that is, the closed shop) required it.

An obsession with "high quality" members, and fear of "dilution" by "raw workers" also came to characterize some of the Trotskyist groups (though not all) and their offshoots. Why is this attitude sectarian? Again we come back to the class struggle as the heart of the matter. And that cuts both ways.

As Trotsky himself wrote: "Coming from the opportunists the accusation of sectarianism is most often a compliment." True enough, but this in no way alters the fact that sectarian deviations can be a real danger. Trotsky explained the emergence of sectarianism amongst some of his followers by the circumstances of their origin.

Every working-class party, every faction, during its initial stages, passes through a period of pure propaganda...The period of existence as a Marxist circle invariably grafts habits of an abstract approach onto the workers' movement. Whoever is unable to step in time over the confines of this circumscribed existence becomes transformed into a conservative sectarian. The sectarian looks upon life as a great school with himself as a teacher there...Though he may swear by Marxism in every sentence the sectarian is the direct negation of dialectical materialism, which takes *experience* as its point of departure and always returns to it...The sectarian lives in a sphere of ready-made formulae...Discord with reality engenders in the sectarian the need to constantly render his formula more precise. This goes under the name of discussion. To a Marxist, discussion is an important but functional instrument of the class struggle. To the sectarian discussion is a goal in itself. However, the more he discusses, the more the actual tasks escape him. He is like a man who satisfies his thirst with salt water; the more he drinks, the thirstier he becomes.

Lenin and the revolutionary party

Tony Cliff

For the achievement of a socialist revolution, a revolutionary party is needed because of the uneven levels of culture and consciousness in different groups of workers. If the working class were homogeneous ideologically, there would be no need for leadership. But the objective possibility of revolution will not wait until all reach a class-conscious intellectual level. Only the revolutionary party can utilize the revolutionary opportunity, given a class only partially aware of its revolutionary tasks.

Unevenness is not static. Sections of the class that are more backward can move ahead quickly, and those formerly in advance fall behind. The sharper and more volatile the struggle, the more relative the terms "advanced" and "backward" become.

The more the revolutionary party is rooted in the working class, the more unevenness in the class affects, and is affected by, unevenness in the party. Different groups of workers are influenced in varying degrees by other classes, and this has its effect on party members. The party's leadership of the working class is the result of struggle against these influences, and inside the party, leadership is secured by fighting for the correct policies. In the same way that a vanguard party is necessary to strengthen the initiative and independence of the mass of workers, democratic centralism inside the party is necessary to develop the initiative and independence of party members.

This, in outline, is Lenin's conception of the revolutionary party, its relationship to the working class, and the form of party organization dictated by that relationship.

However, the norm of party organization—the ideal form—does not correspond with reality. In the norm, the party center—representing the best in the party—is in advance of the localities, committees and branches. Party branches both influence and are influenced by the national leadership. In practice, the position can be very different. A party center can be more advanced than the branches by following a certain routine, which can then result in conservative inertia. If the political situation of the working class changes rapidly, presenting new tasks, the center, being less in touch, can fall behind sections of the party. Different branches of the party react more swiftly than others to the new needs. The more rigid the party structure, the more elaborate its rules, the less adaptable it is to new needs.

Lenin's thoughts and practice contain a number of key elements:

Practice is superior to theory: "Practice is higher than (theoretical) knowledge, for it has not only the dignity of universality, but also of immediate actuality."[1]

Truth is always concrete.

Uneven development of different aspects of the struggle make it necessary to look always to the key link in every concrete situation.[2]

Organization must always be historically determined (not drawn from some "general theory"), and changed to fit major changes in the class struggle.

While the norm of party life is democratic centralist—the central bodies are assumed to be superior in knowledge and initiative—sometimes rules must be broken in the interests of the revolution.

Party rules are means to overcome the anarchic tendencies of individuals and small groups—often recruited from the middle class—but they should not reduce the flexibility of work. At an extreme, breaking party discipline may well be the duty of loyal members.

It is necessary to struggle to avoid empiricism and opportunist indiscipline without falling into dogmatic blind discipline.

Lenin's contribution to showing how a revolutionary party should work is contained in the history of his activity, not in some abstract theory. This article presents some examples to illustrate these points. It does not deal with the whole question of party organization, but with only one aspect: party rules and discipline. The selection of such a narrow field of investigation must lead to one-sidedness. The inner working of the party cannot be understood properly without looking at the relations between the party and the working class.

"What Is to Be Done?"

Lenin's early ideas on organizations were presented in *What Is to Be Done?*, written in 1902. There he argued:

> There could not have been social-democratic consciousness[3] among the workers. It would have to be brought to them from without...The working class, exclusively by its own effort, is able to develop only trade-union consciousness, i.e. the conviction that it is necessary to combine in unions, fight the employers, and strive to compel the government to pass necessary labor legislation.[4]

Furthermore:

> The spontaneous working-class movement is trade unionism...and trade unionism means the ideological enslavement of the workers by the bourgeoisie. Hence our task...is to *combat spontaneity, to divert* the working-class movement from this spontaneous, trade union striving...[5]

> But why...does the spontaneous movement...lead to the domination of bourgeois ideology? For the simple reason that bourgeois ideology is far older in origin than socialist ideology, that it is more fully developed, and that it has at its disposal *immeasurably* more means of dissemination.[6]

The organizational form needed by social-democracy is derived from the nature of the political tasks: "In an autocratic state, the more we *confine* the membership...to people who are professionally engaged in revolutionary activity and who have been professionally trained in the art of combating the political police, the more difficult it will be to unearth the organization."[7]

This orientation was elaborated in a document of 1904. Below the central committee there should be two kinds of groups: territorial and functional (industrial). The local committees "should consist of fully convinced social democrats, who devote themselves entirely to social-democratic activities,"[8] and be small in number. They should direct discussion meetings of revolutionaries, district circles with a propagandists' circle attached to each, factory circles and factory circle delegate meetings. "*All* further institutions (and of these there should be very many and extremely diversified ones...) should be subordinated to the committee, and...it is necessary to have district groups (for the very big cities) and factory groups (always and everywhere)."[9] 'The district groups should be permitted to act independently only on questions concerning the technical aspect of transmission and distribution."[10] Furthermore, "the factory circles...are particularly important to us...: the main strength of the movement lies in the organization of the workers at the *large* factories, for the large factories (and mills) contain not only the predominant part of the working class, as regards numbers, but even more as regards influence, development, and fighting capacity. Every factory must be our fortress."[11]

How did the party machine work in practice?

In practice, things looked very different. Lenin's letters from exile to party committees are full of complaints about the lack of information, literature, and people.[12] "Are you taking workers into the committee?" he asks of the Odessa committee. "This is essential, absolutely essential! Why don't you put us in direct contact with workers? Not a single worker writes to *Vperyod*.[13] *This is a scandal*. We need at all costs *dozens* of worker correspondents."[14] Occasionally, he despairs: "We talk of organization, of centralism, while actually there is such disunity, such amateurism among even the closest comrades in the center, that one feels like chucking it all in disgust."[15]

Early in 1905, we find Krupskaya writing from Geneva to the Petersburg committee: "We learned from foreign papers that the Putilov[16] plant was on strike. Do we have any connections there? Will it really be impossible to get information about the strike?" Nevskii comments:

> One of the greatest proletarian movements was beginning, already its spearhead—the Putilov workers—was fighting capitalists, but the center abroad learned of these clashes from foreign papers...it was not even able to sense that the strike...was...a movement linked by the closest ties to... the whole mighty strike movement of the entire Petersburg proletariat.[17]

At the third party congress, the Petersburg committee admitted:

> The January events *[the wave of mass strikes that marked the start of the 1905 revolution—Ed.]* caught the Petersburg committee in an extremely sorry state. Its ties with the working masses had been utterly disorganized... There was not a single worker among the members of the committee. The strike at the Putilov plant caught the committee unprepared.[18]

As a result of its weakness, inexperience, and shallow roots in the working class, the Bolshevik committee was a natural prey to ultra-left sectarianism during 1905—symbolized by its rejection of the soviet when established.

A similar sectarian attitude was shown by the Bolshevik leadership in Russia towards the newly-rising trade unions. As in the case of the soviet, Lenin had to fight his own democratic centralist leadership in alliance with the party rank and file. The 1905 revolution showed clearly that the party is not automatically in advance of the class, nor the central committee in advance of the party.

Tactical turns

Theoretically, the party member was a professional revolutionary, a "committeeman." In the period before the 1905 revolution (and in the years of reaction after it), the committeemen were far in advance of the level of activity and consciousness of even the advanced section of the proletariat. But in the revolution, they lagged far behind. In the difficult years of illegality and repression, the committeemen created a routine, a tradition, which at the moment of crisis became an impediment.

During 1905, the main theme of Lenin's argument was: open the gates of the party to new forces.

> Really, I sometimes think that nine-tenths of the Bolsheviks are actually formalists... We need young forces. I am for shooting on the spot anyone who presumes to say that there are no people to be had. The people in Russia are legion; all we have to do is to recruit young people...*without fearing them...*
>
> Enlarge the committee *threefold* by accepting young people into it, set up half a dozen or a dozen subcommittees, "co-opt" any and every honest and energetic person. Allow every subcommittee to write and publish leaflets without any red tape (there is no harm if they do make a mistake...)...Do not fear their lack of training, do not tremble at their inexperience and lack of development...[19]

And again:

> If we fail to show bold initiative in setting up new organizations, we shall have to give up as groundless all pretensions to the role of vanguard. If we stop helplessly at the achieved boundaries, forms, and confines of the committees, groups, meetings and circles, we shall merely prove our own

incapacity. Thousands of circles are now springing up everywhere without our aid, without any definite program or aim, simply under the impact of events.

Let all such circles, except those that are avowedly non-social-democratic, either directly join the party or *align themselves to the party*. In the latter event we must not demand that they accept our program or that they necessarily enter into organizational relations with us. Their mood of protest and their sympathy for the cause of international revolutionary social-democracy in themselves suffice.[20]

However, the committeemen opposed Lenin's appeal, and at the third congress (in the spring of 1905), defeated him on the issue. The admission of new workers to the party aroused particular opposition. One delegate argued that the problem did not exist: "As an issue of the relationship of workers and the intelligentsia to party organizations, this question does not exist (Lenin: 'yes it does.') No, it does not: it exists as a demagogic question, that is all."[21] Others reported how few workers actually were committee members—one in Petersburg after 15 years work (Lenin: "Outrageous!"), none on the northern committee, one in Baku, none in Kutais. The complaints followed thick and fast. One delegate remarked: "In our committees—and I have seen plenty of them in my work—there is some kind of phobia towards workers."[22]

At this point Lenin intervened, and the session became even noisier:

It will be the task of the future center to reorganize a considerable number of our committees: the inertness of the committeemen has to be overcome (applause and booing)...To place workers on the committees is a political, not only a pedagogical, task. Workers have class instinct, and, given some political experience, they pretty soon become staunch social-democrats. I should be strongly in favor of having eight workers to every two intellectuals on our committees.[23]

Mikhailov developed the point further:

The criterion for admitting workers...ought to be different from the one applied to the intelligentsia. There is talk of tempered social democrats, but...first- and second-year students, familiar with social-democratic ideas from the Erfurt Program and a few issues of *Iskra*, are already considered tempered social-democrats. Thus in practice the requirements for intelligentsia are very low, and for workers they are extremely high. (Lenin: "Very true!" The majority of delegates: "Not True!") The only valid criterion for admitting workers into committee must be the degree of their influence among the masses (hissing, shouting). All workers who are leaders and have been in our circles must be members of our committees.[24]

Lenin returned to the subject later:

A tight hold must always be kept on the intelligentsia. It is always the instigator of all sorts of squabbles...Clause nine (of the constitution): A local committee must be dissolved by the central committee if two-thirds of the local workers belonging to the party organizations declare for such a dissolution...when our central committee is constantly posted on the number of workers organized in any particular organization, it will have to reckon with their opinion and will be bound to cashier the local committee on the demand of the organized workers.[25]

It was not the last time Lenin found himself in a minority among the Bolshevik leaders, and even booed at a Bolshevik congress. Yet he continued to argue against the leadership. Later in the year, we find him saying:

At the third congress of the party I suggested that there be about eight workers to every two intellectuals in the party committees. How obsolete that suggestion seems today! Now we must wish for the party organizations to have one social-democratic intellectual to several hundred social-democratic workers.[26]

And a year later:

It is abnormal that we should have only 6,000 party members in St. Petersburg (in St. Petersburg district there are 81,000 workers in factories employing 500 or more workers, 150,000 workers in all)...We must learn to recruit five times and 10 times as many workers for the party in such centers.[27]

Lenin had to protect his followers from allegiance to *What Is to Be Done?* His formulation there of the relationship between spontaneity and organization still bedevils the movement. Yet in 1905 he clearly reversed his position:

The working class is instinctively, spontaneously social-democratic... extend your bases, rally all the worker social-democrats round yourselves, incorporate them in the ranks of the party organizations by hundreds and thousands.[28]

The zigzags that led Lenin into conflict with the rest of the party leadership would have destroyed the party if Lenin had not insisted, from the beginning, that party rules be few in number and flexible in character.

Against red tape: for very general party rules

Lenin regarded party rules as matters of convenience, not something that ought to take great time and thought:

> What is needed is not rules but the organization of party information... Each of our local organizations now spend at least a few evenings on discussing rules. If instead, each member would devote this time to making a detailed and well-prepared report *to the entire party* on his particular function, the work would gain a hundredfold.[29]

When he formulated the party rules in 1903, they were extremely simple and few—12 rules, presented in 421 words. Yet even so, he found it necessary to break them on occasion.

Contrary to Lenin's wishes, the new central committee—wholly Bolshevik after 1903—began to try to conciliate the Mensheviks.[30] After months of acrimonious correspondence, Lenin was to all intents and purposed ousted from the committee, which then recognized the authority of the wholly Menshevik *Iskra* editorial board.[31] The committee denounced Lenin's agitation for a new congress to settle accounts with the Mensheviks and dissolved the southern bureau. Lenin was deprived of his position as the central committee's foreign representative, and his writings were not to be published without the committee's sanction.

The southern bureau had been created by Lenin behind the back of the committee; it had no official status and served as Lenin's mouthpiece in the call for new congress.

Lenin now set about organizing a new network of disciplined followers in Russia, regardless of rule six, which vested the right to organize committees solely in the central committee. With this organization, he called for a new congress, a direct violation of the party statutes he himself had drawn up.

Take another example. At the Stockholm "unification" congress (1906), the Mensheviks gained a majority on the central committee. Would Lenin now stick to the rule that local branches or committees of the party should be subordinate to the committee? Not at all. Now he called for autonomy of party branches in deciding their *own* political line, and referenda of the members to replace decisions of the central bodies.

At the third conference of the Russian Social-Democratic Workers Party (held in July 1907), in which Bolsheviks as well as Mensheviks were represented, a curious situation arose: all the Bolshevik delegates, with the sole exception of Lenin, voted in favor of boycotting the elections to the Duma. Lenin voted with the Mensheviks.[32] At the 1907 London congress of the united party, where Lenin got his way on practically every issue, an overwhelming vote was passed against armed robberies and expropriations in the interests of the party. A majority of the Bolsheviks voted with the Mensheviks. When delegates shouted: "What does Lenin say? We want to hear Lenin," he, taking advantage of his position as chairman, avoided registering his vote—he only chuckled "with a somewhat cryptic expression."[33] A month after the London congress, and notwithstanding its resolutions, Lenin's agents carried out the most audacious expropriation ever, that of the Tiflis treasury—netting 341,000 rubles!

Or take the expulsion of Bogdanov, the leader of the "Left Bolsheviks." In 1909, the party was split, and any attempt to call a conference or congress would probably have resulted in its destruction. The decline of the movement in the years of reaction had led to demoralization. Lenin regarded the removal of Bogdanov, elected to the old Bolshevik center at the 1906 London congress, as vital for the restoration of the party. Accordingly he summoned an entirely *ad hoc* body—an enlarged editorial board meeting of the Bolshevik journal *Proletary*—and expelled Bogdanov. Lenin could not turn to active workers to get support for his stand against Bogdanov, so he made use of a very unrepresentative body for the same end. Many of Lenin's supporters—even Stalin—criticized this apparently arbitrary act. He was wrong formally, but he saved Bolshevism from extinction in an ultra-left void.

Ultra-leftism thrives when revolutionaries are isolated from any real support in the working class. Since practically nobody is listening, why not resort to extreme revolutionary phrasemongering? Ultra-leftists are formalistic, sterile and out of touch with reality—but how can one prove this without mass action? Lenin cut the knot by breaking the rules: organizational principles, for him, were always subordinate to concrete political tasks and what he saw as the main priority of the moment.

How did Lenin survive conflicts with his own supporters?

Even taking into account the fact that we are not describing the political background of these events, nor the highly regular and disciplined nature of the rest of Bolshevik work, it might seem surprising that Lenin managed to survive as party leader. There were five main reasons for this:

1. The proletarian composition of the party. In 1905, workers were a majority of the party (62 percent[34]). In the period of reaction, intellectuals left the party in droves; few returned in the years of revival (1912 to 1914). A new exodus took place during the war years, so the Bolsheviks became more and more proletarianized in composition.

2. The youth of the party. In 1907, 22 percent of the party members were less than 20 years old; 37 percent were between 20 and 24, and 16 percent between 25 and 29. "Activists"—defined as propagandists, public speakers, agitators or members of armed party detachments—were scarcely older. 17 percent were under 20; 42 percent between 20 and 24, and 24 percent between 25 and 29. Delegates to the fifth congress of 1907 had an average age of 27. The average age of the nine leaders was 34 (and of the three eldest—Krasin, Lenin and Krasikov—37).[35]

The young were the innovators, self-sacrificing and energetic. They made it easier for Lenin to overcome the conservative resistance of the party.

3. Lenin's reliance on the advanced sections of the class. Lenin knew that an overformal party structure inevitably clashed with the unevenness of consciousness and militancy within the revolutionary movement and within the party—so that some who had played the role of vanguard at one stage, fell behind at another. Lenin always looked to the advanced section of party workers for support against the conservatives.

At the time of the February revolution of 1917, the Petrograd soviet's executive had 11 Bolsheviks among its 39 members, yet no one opposed the formation of a bourgeois government. Stalin and Kamenev, returning from exile in Siberia, also supported the provisional government and ended the anti-war policies of the Bolsheviks. The party rank and file was much less unanimous. The Vyborg district in particular—an area of medium engineering and a well-organized Bolshevik base—publicly opposed the leaders, and called—in meetings attended by thousands of workers and soldiers—for soviet power.[36] Vyborg Bolsheviks demanded that the soviets immediately seize power and abolish the Assembly's provisional committee.[37] However, the Petrograd committee banned the resolution, and the Vyborg district was forced to submit.

It was the support of the Vyborg Bolsheviks and other rank-and-file members that made it possible for Lenin to win the party so swiftly to his April Theses. When he first wrote them, he had no support among the leadership:

> Not one Bolshevik organization or group or even individual had joined him... "As for Lenin's general scheme," wrote *Pravda*, "it seems to us unacceptable, insofar as it proceeds from the assumption that the bourgeois-democratic revolution is finished and counts on the immediate conversion of that revolution into a socialist revolution."[38]

Kamenev wrote in the paper that neither *Pravda* nor the bureau of the central committee accepted Lenin's position.

Yet within two weeks, the tide was turning. The Petrograd city conference overwhelmingly endorsed Lenin's condemnation of the provisional government, and a national Bolshevik conference then went on to do the same.[39] In terms of formal democracy, Petrograd with its two million people, and even more the Vyborg district with its 170,000, were tiny minorities in the country. But in a period of revolutionary crisis, particular groups can have a disproportionate impact on the course of history. The Petrograd Bolsheviks might accept the April Theses; elsewhere Bolsheviks continued in alliance with the Mensheviks until July or August 1917. To give equal weight to Petrograd Bolsheviks and—say—Kharkov or Odessa Bolsheviks, would have meant adaptation to the backward.

4. The structure of the party. The leading bodies of the party—congresses, conferences, central committees—were quite small in size. For example, the 1903 conference had 57 delegates; the 1907 conference had 336 delegates (for 46,000 members); the April 1917 conference had 149 delegates (for 200,000 members). Prior to 1917, the central committee varied between three and 12 members; there were 22 at the time of the October Revolution, when the party had 270,000 members.

The congresses were long. The second (1903) lasted 25 days; the third (1905) 16 days; the fourth (1906) 16 days; the fifth (1907) 20 days, and the sixth (1917) nine days. The small size of congresses and the length of time for which they met guaranteed serious debate on the real issues facing the party, strengthened its internal democracy, and helped keep it stable. A large conference held for a short time is more easily manipulated.

Long-lived factions were a rare phenomenon. The reason was not only the proletarian composition of the party, but also the institutional arrangements at congresses. Bogdanov's was the longest lasting faction. It came into being at a time when the party was quite isolated from the working class, and lasted some three years.

5. Lenin as an administer who detested red tape. Lenin was unique among revolutionary leaders in his careful attention to administrative detail. How unusual this was becomes evident if we compare him with, for example, the Polish Social-Democrats:

> To a large extent each member of the elite acted on his own initiative and in accordance with his own predilections and habits. Orders were rare indeed; apart from exceptional cases...this haphazard informality was deliberate and jealously guarded. Some of the leaders very much disliked having to deal with money and organizational routine at all; it kept them from their writing...The same applied even more strongly to Rosa Luxemburg. At some stage a formal party decision was reached that she should not concern herself with organizational matters at all, that she should not participate in any of the official conferences or congresses.[40]

Similarly, Trotsky was not involved in party administration, but for different reasons. He did not belong to any real party between 1904, when he broke with the Mensheviks, and 1917, when he joined the Bolsheviks.

The Bolshevik administrative center was most primitive. There were only three people in the secretariat during the 1905 revolution. This penny-ha'penny apparatus, together with conditions of illegality and the proletarian composition of the party, made it practically impossible for petty-bourgeois factionalism to develop. The party member was expected to participate in determining the general line of the party and to know the *specific* job he himself had to do. There was no place for the intense gossip group.

Lenin's undogmatic attitude to centralism

A revolutionary party cannot intervene effectively in working-class struggles unless it is centralized and acts as a disciplined body. It cannot be sensitive to the needs of the advanced workers unless it is consistently democratic. Between the revolutionary party and the class, between centralism and democracy, there is a dialectical relationship. If one position is pushed to an extreme, it is possible to fall from the despotism of the common man to the impotence of the phrasemonger. Lenin was always ready to strengthen the central bodies, but without forgetting the initiative, in the final analysis, lies with the masses, and the task of the party is not to stifle it but to raise it.

Lenin knew that organization had to be subordinated to politics. His genius in the field of revolutionary practice—in strategy and tactics—was the real pillar that established his hegemony in the party. Scientific understanding of the general movement of history, fortified by great sensitivity to the moods and aspirations of the workers, gave Lenin extreme confidence that the path he chose was right. Under such circumstances, of course, organizational rules and regulations appeared to him as of secondary importance to practice. Without the correctness of his conclusions, the "indiscipline" of Lenin would have been on more than simple arbitrariness and caprice. Walking the narrow line between dogmatism and empiricism, Lenin developed the practical essence of Marxism—including the question of organization—to the highest concreteness ever achieved.

1   V. I. Lenin, *Collected Works, Volume 38*, (Moscow, 1965), p. 213 (Henceforth *CW*, followed by volume number and page).

2   Tony Cliff, "From Marxist circle to agitation," *International Socialism 52*, July-September 1972, p. 16.

3   "Social-democratic." The Marxist working-class parties of Europe were usually called "social-democratic" before 1914, so "social-democratic" roughly refers to organized Marxists, as does "social-democracy."

4   *CW*, 5, p. 375.

5   Ibid, p. 384.

6   Ibid, p. 386.

7   Ibid, p. 464.

8   Letter to a comrade on our organizational tasks, *CW*, 6, p. 250.

9   Ibid, p. 238.

10   Ibid, p. 24.1

11   *CW*, 6, p. 245.

12   For example, see letters of 15 August 1904, *CW* 34, p. 245; 12 July 1905, *CW* 34, p. 319; 29 January; 1905, *CW* 34, p. 283 and p. 323.

13   *Vperyod* (Forward): illegal Bolshevik weekly, directed by Lenin and published in Geneva from December 1904 to May 1905.

14   *CW*, 34, p. 307.

15   Letter to Bogdanov and Gusev, 11 February 1905, *CW* 8, p. 145.

16   Putilov: the famous Petrograd machinery plant, a stronghold of Bolshevism.

17   V Nevskii, *Rabochee dvizhenie v ianarskie* dni v. Peterburgev 1905. 3, Moscow, 1922, p. 88, 157.

18   *Tretii s'ezd RSDRP, Apre'-mai goda, Protokoly*, Moscow, Gospolitizdat, 1959, p. 544-5.

19   *CW*, 8, p. 219/420.

20   *Tretii*, op. cit., p. 255.

21   Ibid, p. 257.

22   Ibid, p. 355.

23   *CW*, 8, p. 408.

24   *Tretii*, p. 262.

25   *CW*, 8, p. 416.

26   *CW*, 10, p. 36.

27   *CW*, 11, p. 358-9.

28   *CW*, 10, p. 32.

29   *CW*, 6, p. 252.

30   The major split in the Russian Social-Democratic Workers Party was between the Bolsheviks and the Mensheviks. It began at the second congress in 1903 and, although numerous reunification attempts were made, remained permanent. The Mensheviks were only loosely affiliated to each other; they were intellectuals, with numerous different currents. The Bolsheviks aimed to build a disciplined and centralized party.

31   *Iskra* (The Spark): the first all-Russian illegal Marxist newspaper, founded abroad by Lenin in 1900 and smuggled into Russia. After the second congress, the Mensheviks (see last note) gained control of the paper—known as the "new" *Iskra.*

32   *VKkP v rezoliutsiyakh I resheniyakh sedov, konferentsii I plenumov tsk,* volume 1, Moscow 1954, p. 126.

33   L. Trotsky, *My Life,* New York, 1960, p. 218.

34   Bolshevik membership in 1905: Workers: 5,200 (61.9%); Peasants: 400 (4.8%); White-collar: 2,300 (27.4%); Others: 500 (5.9%); Total: 8,400. Cited by David Lane, *The Roots of Russian Communism,* London, 1970, p. 21.

35   Calculated from Lane, *Ibid.,* p. 37.

36   Sukhanov, N.N., *The Russian Revolution 1917,* London, 1955, p. 107-8, and F. N. Dingelstadt, *Krasnaya letopis,* No. 1 (12), 1925.

37   *KPSS v borbe za pobedu sotsialisticheskoi revolyutsii v period dvovlastii 27 fevralya—4 iylya 1917 g. Sbornik dokumentov.* Moscow 1951 p. 172.

38   Sukhanov, *op. cit.,* p. 299.

39   *VKP v rez op. cit.* p. 339.

40   J.P. Nettl, *Rosa Luxemburg,* London, 1966, volume 1, p. 263-5.

About Haymarket Books

Haymarket Books is a radical, independent, nonprofit book publisher based in Chicago.

Our mission is to publish books, particularly new and classical works of Marxism, that contribute to struggles for social and economic justice. We strive to make our books a vibrant and organic part of social movements and the education and development of a critical, engaged, international left.

We take inspiration and courage from our namesakes, the Haymarket martyrs, who gave their lives fighting for a better world. Their 1886 struggle for the eight-hour day—which gave us May Day, the international workers' holiday—reminds workers around the world that ordinary people can organize and struggle for their own liberation. These struggles continue today across the globe—struggles against oppression, exploitation, poverty, and war.

Since our founding in 2001, Haymarket Books has published more than five hundred titles. Radically independent, we seek to drive a wedge into the risk-averse world of corporate book publishing. Our authors include Eqbal Ahmad, Arundhati Roy, Angela Y. Davis, Howard Zinn, Ian Birchall, Ahmed Shawki, Paul Le Blanc, Mike Davis, Kim Scipes, Ilan Pappé, Michael Roberts, Sharon Smith, Dave Zirin, Keeanga-Yamahtta Taylor, Nick Turse, Kim Moody, Danny Katch, Jeffery R. Webber, Paul D'Amato, Amira Hass, Sherry Wolf, Naomi Klein, and Neil Davidson. We are also the trade publishers of the acclaimed Historical Materialism Book Series, and of the Studies in Critical Social Sciences book series, as well as Dispatch Books.

Shop our full catalog online at www.haymarketbooks.org.

About the authors

Tony Cliff (1917–2000) was a lifelong organizer within the international socialist movement. His groundbreaking work helped establish the interpretation of the Soviet Union as a bureaucratic, state-centered version of capitalism, rather than a workers' state. His many works include *State Capitalism in Russia, Building the Party* and *All Power To the Soviets*.

Duncan Hallas (1925–2002) was born in Manchester, and joined the Trotskyist Workers International League during World War II. Over the course of his career, he was consistently active in his teachers' union and elsewhere. During the great upheaval of 1968 he rejoined the International Socialists. From that time on he was a leading member of the organization, a great popularizer of Marxism and an inspired speaker, until ill health forced him out of active politics in 1995. Hallas's many essays and books include *Trotsky's Marxism*, published by Haymarket Books in 2003.

Chris Harman (1942–2009) was a leading member of the Socialist Workers Party (UK) and the editor of *Socialist Worker* (UK) newspaper. He is the author of many books, articles and pamphlets, including *A People's History of the World, Class Struggles in Eastern Europe, The Fire Last Time: 1968 and After, Economics of the Madhouse, How Marxism Works* and *Zombie Capitalism*.

Leon Trotsky (1879–1940) was a key leader of the Russian Revolution. Forced into exile in 1928, Trotsky devoted the rest of his life to fighting the degeneration of the revolution and rise of a new dictatorial regime. Vilified and isolated, he fought an uncompromising battle with the Stalinist bureaucracy, defending the revolutionary and internationalist principles upon which the revolution was based. In 1940, he was murdered by an agent of the Stalinist regime.